Can the Law of Attraction Be Made Easy?

By Austin Blake Wintergreen

Copyright © 2020 by Austin Wintergreen – All Rights Reserved

This book or any portion thereof may not be reproduced or used in any manner whatsoever without the publisher's express written permission except for the use of a brief quotation in a book review.

Edgar Quicksand & Sons Book Publishing
Scottsdale, Arizona

Interior Layout by Sandeep Likhar
Cover Design by Gus Tikno

www.AustinWintergreen.com

Note from the author

Dear Reader,

Thank you for your interest in this book. I greatly appreciate it. This is my second book, and I am incredibly happy to have found an audience I can help.

May I ask you a favor?

If you should encounter any spelling or grammatical errors that bother you, could you email me personally before expressing your disappointment on Amazon?

I put a lot of effort into making sure this second book is free of errors, but some are bound to get through. In addition to hiring professional proofreaders, I've also meticulously proofread this book over nine times. However…

When I reviewed this book on Grammarly, there were still some mistakes! This can be so frustrating as an author. As a reader, it can be equally frustrating to read a book that has spelling and grammatical errors.

So, if you could let me know about any spelling or grammatical errors, I'd greatly appreciate it. This way, I can fix them right away so others won't get frustrated. Here is my email address: AustinWintergreen@Gmail.com

Best wishes,

Austin Wintergreen

7 Suggestions to Getting the Most Out of This Book

1. Develop a deep, burning desire to change your current circumstance.
2. Read each chapter carefully, visualizing how your life will change.
3. As you read, pause for a moment, and see how you can apply what you have learned.
4. Apply these principles as often as you can.
5. Be open to tactics and strategies that you have not heard before.
6. Understand that you will have a monumental mind shift.
7. Read this book entirely before reading any other book. Success through total focus.

Table of Contents

Preface: Why I Wrote This Book 7

Introduction: Tapping Into the Law of Attraction 15

Chapter 1: Manifesting Marriage in 7 Days by Letting Go 21

Chapter 2: Are Your Law of Attraction Tactics Helping or
Hurting Your Success? 33

Chapter 3: Discover the Deep-Rooted Blocks That Are Keeping
You from Abundant Success 47

Chapter 4: The Big Secret on How Manifesting Works 57

Chapter 5: Why the Universe Gives You What You Want 71

Chapter 6: Discover the Riddle of the Abundance or
Contraction Mindset 89

Chapter 7: If Positive Thinking Hasn't Worked for You, Read This 101

Chapter 8: The One Ingredient Hidden Inside You for
Ultimate Success 125

Chapter 9: The Short-Cut to Raising Your Vibration and
Allowing All Your Desires to Flow to You Quickly 139

Chapter 10: 9 Practical Exercises to Quickly Manifest
Your Most Elusive Desires 155

Conclusion 181

Preface:
Why I Wrote This Book

Several years ago, I had come down with a viral infection that had me in the hospital for a day. The doctors and nurses did an excellent job of fixing me up. Upon my arrival, my head felt like it would explode from all the pressure building up inside. I just wanted to drill a hole anywhere in my head to release the pressure. My skin all over my body was ravished with red welts. Blood was coming out of my eyes. My wonderful wife left work to take me to the hospital. I was so grateful to have such a wonderful woman in my life.

Sitting on the hospital bed, the nurses gave me every kind of drug and medication to relieve all the pain and discomfort. I was so grateful for that. To make an exceptionally long story short, they gave me a round of antibiotics and sent me home.

Heart palpitations

For four straight years after my illness and hospital visit, I had consistent and debilitating heart palpitations. Many times, it felt like a wild animal jumping around in the center of my chest. Other times—more than I can count—I felt like I would die right where I stood. I had hundreds of these episodes. In my mind, I was on the brink of death hundreds of times a day. It was scary and nerve-wracking.

Sometimes my heart would flutter. Sometimes it would just stop for a split second and then start again. Other times it would beat so fast that it felt like I had run a marathon or a 50-yard dash. It was scary. I didn't think my heart would be able to take it anymore.

During these SVT episodes, I would clutch my chest and just wondered when my heart was going to give out. SVT stands for Supraventricular Tachycardia. These episodes can happen out of nowhere. Sometimes, I would sit at my desk working on a project, and then my heart would beat at nearly 200 beats per minute or more. A normal pulse (heart rhythm) is anywhere from 60 beats per minute to 100 beats per minute. My normal pulse at my age is 60 beats per minute. So, when these SVT episodes happened, it was quite a shock to my system.

I would have many of these episodes throughout the week. When I didn't have a full-on SVT episode with a rapid heart rate, I would have other kinds of heart palpitations. These are called PVCs (premature ventricular contractions) and PACs (premature atrial contractions), just to name a few. There are many more heart arrhythmias, but those are the ones I suffered from the most.

Most people have heard of AFib, which is short for arterial fibrillation. Without getting too technical, these are all similar. Basically, the heart isn't beating normally. It's erratic. However, it's not an indication of heart disease, as most people would think. It's an electrical/nerve problem rather than a clogged artery problem.

While many doctors will tell their patients that these heart arrhythmias are harmless, these erratic heartbeats can be quite frightening. Personally, whenever I had a heart palpitation of any kind, I felt like I was going to die.

When other parts of your body have pain or don't feel right, you have a slight concern. However, when it's your heart, you think of the worst.

Naturally, this would heighten your anxiety. I never had anxiety before the onset of these heart episodes. But since I was reminded about a hundred times a day that I could die at any moment, I started to get a little anxious.

After going to many doctors and having several emergency room visits, I realized that I needed to find a solution. It took me about six months to find a solution I could live with for the rest of my life.

The solution

The solution I wrote about in my two previous books is that it's all in my head. Many doctors had told me that my heart palpitations were all in my head, but they didn't provide a way for me to overcome this.

And let me be clear by what I mean by it's all in my head. It doesn't mean I am crazy or that I *think* I'm having a heart palpitation. I know I'm having a heart palpitation. I'm not dreaming it. Even a doctor's office visit would confirm this. It just means that there is no physical source for my heart palpitations—such as heart disease.

It was all anxiety, as my doctors told me. However, I had a hard time believing this because I didn't have any anxiety at all. I was very calm and relaxed.

It took me four long years to find a solution. The solution was to fix my head. The significant side effect of finding a solution was that I had confirmed that I could—through thought alone—make changes to my body. I had the power to make changes by thought alone. Knowing this was a big breakthrough for me.

I had heard about the Law of Attraction over 14 years ago and investigated it. Unfortunately, I read too many articles from naysayers who said it was a bunch of nonsense. Therefore, I abandoned the idea.

However, since I cured my heart palpitations—a real physical disorder—through my thoughts, I had a new appreciation for the Law of Attraction and changing oneself through thought alone.

Changing my thoughts

One of the things that I did to cure my heart palpitations was to repeat a mantra. That mantra went something like this: "I have a strong and healthy heart, and I feel great." I repeated that over and over.

Slowly but surely, my heart palpitations started to go away. This was a big breakthrough for me. I believed that I could change matter with my mind. It was mind over matter.

I started to apply the same methodology to other parts of my life. I would repeat little mantras to myself and found I could manifest different things in my life. However, the biggest realization was that I always had the power to manifest things all my life. I just didn't realize it.

When I started to look back at my history, I realized how much stuff I had manifested in my life just through thought alone.

Later, I will discuss a concept called "dancing with life" and going with the flow. That was the way I lived when I was young, and things came to me naturally. It wasn't until I was an adult with all the responsibilities and fears that I started to lose my magic touch.

On the search to resolve my heart palpitations issues, I came across many "mind over matter" gurus. Dr. Joe Dispenza is one of the leaders who demonstrate how you can use your mind to shape matter. I learned so much from him, and I owe him a debt of gratitude. Because of his teachings, I was able to overcome a very debilitating disorder. It was ruining my life, and no doctor was giving me any real answers. And no one else seemed to have a solution either.

Since I resolved my heart palpitations through thought alone, I wanted to help others resolve their issues. Therefore, I wrote two books about doing just that. I won't get into details about those books. If you're interested, you can just check them out on Amazon. Anyway, I wanted to give back. I wanted to help people the same way Dr. Joe Dispenza helped me.

Too much B.S.

For this book, I wanted to help steer people in the right direction. Through trial and error, I found a lot of the information about manifesting and the Law of Attraction was just a lot of B.S.

I wanted to dispel many myths surrounding the Law of Attraction and the act of manifesting things into your life. I found a lot of B.S. and B.S. gurus and practitioners. A lot of what they teach was not only wrong and destructive but also needlessly confusing and obfuscating.

This book will clear up some of the confusion that I have found so rampant. There are some extremely popular Law of Attraction gurus who are especially and needlessly confusing. I doubt that they ever actually manifested anything in their lives—other than being some LOA guru. I find them very distasteful.

On the other hand, I learned a lot from other people who teach about manifesting things into your life. These gurus have been instrumental in allowing me to finetune my abilities to shape my life the way I want. I owe a great deal of gratitude to them. If it weren't for them, I wouldn't be where I am today.

I am grateful to have found them. Not only for the wisdom to manifest things into my life but also for giving me a whole new attitude about life. Before I stumbled upon many of these practitioners, I was a sad, lonely, and angry person. I would lash out a lot online. I would make nasty comments on Facebook. I would give terrible reviews of books and products on Amazon.

Since studying and practicing the Law of Attraction, I have mellowed out tremendously. I am now more—much more—kinder and gentler.

New attitude

When I started to be kinder and gentler, things changed for me. When I stopped complaining all the time, things changed for me. When I stopped blaming other people for my problems, things changed for me.

My life changed when I stopped giving bad reviews and started giving constructive criticism. I no longer give anything less than a five-star review on Amazon. If I don't like something, I just keep it to myself. The only exception is if there is a serious defect in a product. However, if that is the case, everyone else would give less than five stars, so it just cancels itself out.

For books, I realized that it's all personal. I often try to avoid reading reviews of books because I want things to unfold naturally without any expectations. This how we did it in "the olden days." You went to a bookstore and just started reading a book. If it grabbed ya, you bought it. If not, you put it back on the shelf. You didn't shout from the rooftops, telling the world how much a book sucks.

I now always finish a book even if I don't particularly like it. My massive action and ability to follow through have resulted in massive changes in my life. I am no longer depressed, and I have an enormous sense of pride. People around me have noticed a difference.

Now, I love it when Amazon sends me an email asking me to review a product or book. I take great pride in doing so. It's like putting a penny in my bank account.

I hope you enjoy this book as much as I had experiencing it.

Okay, who are we kidding? Reading a book about manifesting good things in your life isn't nearly as satisfying as actually manifesting good things in your life. I hope you get out of this book what I hope you will get out of it. You will get a lot of lessons, stories, analogies, anecdotes, and other treats.

Enjoy!

Introduction: Tapping Into the Law of Attraction

You have the power

You have the power to have anything you want. It's true. I've seen amazing things happen many times myself. If you have a willingness to believe, then you have the power to make things happen.

If you have patience, you will succeed beyond your wildest dreams. Okay, maybe I'm exaggerating a little bit. However, if you learn a few simple tricks, you will discover that you can have the life you have always wanted and deserve. The critical question is, "Do you know what you want?"

We will explore this critical question and other concepts throughout this book. Soon, you will be on your way to discovering the magic within you. The beautiful thing about this kind of magic is that the more you know, the more you affect changes in your life. Learning is vital, so be sure to read all the chapters thoroughly before skipping to the Practical Exercises in the back of the book.

Not taking the time to learn is the biggest problem for people trying to manifest a better life. They don't have enough knowledge. If this is you, then you are on the right track. This book will dispel many of the myths surrounding this practical magic. You will learn how to manifest things just by focusing your energy in the right direction.

Unconventional ideas

This book will explore many concepts you may not have heard anywhere else. Some ideas will be familiar to you, and some may not. Even still, you will encounter some familiar concepts with a new twist for added success.

You will learn about how the Universe works and how it's all within you. We'll answer the age-old question: "Am I doing all this, or is the Universe delivering all this to me?" It's an interesting question. Many people have their opinions. All those who have had massive success with manifesting their dream lives have come to the same conclusion.

In the chapters ahead, you will hear stories of love and marriage, jobs gained and lost, dream homes acquired, and incredible coincidences and synchronicities.

Have the right tools

There are tools you should use regularly and tools that you should avoid at all costs. Of course, this may be a matter of opinion, but I will show you many examples where the most popular strategies for manifesting have backfired—and how I did the exact opposite for great success.

At any rate, you need to take this magic stuff seriously. If you don't, you will find things that don't go your way, and you will surely be disappointed.

When I was "dabbling" in magic, I asked for $7,800 to see if the Universe was listening to me. It was. $7,800 was in my future, but not in the way that I had planned. We will discuss that powerful connection with the Universe in a later chapter.

You'll also see how I asked for a big backyard where I didn't have to do much maintenance. Instead, I got a house with a small yard sitting next to a picturesque private golf course. I have a great view and don't have to do a lot of maintenance. This is exactly what I wanted to manifest. Who knew it would come in this form! Let's find out in the chapters ahead.

Removing Blocks

If you want to be super successful in your manifestations, you must remove the blocks that keep your desires from you. Much of this manifestation comes down to removing blocks you have about money, love, success, and relationships. This book will go into detail about the mechanics of all that. It's a simple formula:

1. *Remove blocks*
2. *Ask for what you want*
3. *Set it free*
4. *Don't be attached to the outcome*
5. *See it appear before you in the most unexpected ways*

One of the biggest reasons why some people can manifest more quickly than others is that they are more in touch with their true selves. They have removed their blocks and believe they are worthy of whatever they receive. We will explore this in more detail later in the book.

There are plenty of analogies, examples, and stories in this book, so you will gain a deep understanding of how all this manifesting stuff works. Once you see these examples, you will understand what everyone is talking about when they refer to "manifesting" or "connecting to the Universe" or "having gratitude." It's all spelled out for you here in this book.

Bridges

You will discover what I call "bridges." These are little anecdotes that will *bridge* the gap in your understanding of how all this manifestation stuff and the Universe works. In this book, you will read about these bridges. The *Aunt & Uncle Bridge* has you imagining giving gifts to your nieces and nephews. This will deepen your understanding of how the Universe gives you the things you ask for.

You will discover the *Big Hollywood Movie Producer Bridge*, which will give you a new perspective on how the Universe gives you what's best for you—not necessarily what you ask for.

The *Desert Island Bridge* will challenge your concept of what it means to be happy and have everything you always wanted.

These bridges in understanding will allow you to quickly comprehend what you are doing wrong and correct your mistakes.

Opportunities

Before long, you will manifest a golden opportunity for a wonderful job that you love. You will manifest a love interest that will lead to marriage. You will manifest the home of your dreams. All of these are yours when you genuinely understand how the Universe works.

It's essential to think of your manifestations as opportunities because sometimes, you won't recognize what you have manifested right away. If you don't understand it for what it is, it may pass you by. Some manifestations are apparent and will hit you like a ton of bricks. Some are less obvious, so you must have complete knowledge of how the Universe works.

Looking back, it's easy to see where you came from, but it's hard to know where you are going.

> *"You can't connect the dots looking forward; you can only connect them looking backward. So, you have to trust that the dots will somehow connect in your future. You have to trust in something – your gut, destiny, life, karma, whatever. Because believing that the dots will connect down the road will give you the confidence to follow your heart even when it leads you off the well-worn path, and that will make all the difference."*
> —Steve Jobs, Stanford commencement speech, 2005.

Think of opportunities instead of stuff. Yes, you can manifest things, but it may not be in the form you had envisioned. Many spiritual teachers advocate manifesting money because it's recognizable. You'll know it when you see it. You may not realize that you are living in the perfect house for you until you've lived in it for a while. You may not understand that you indeed manifested the ideal job until the right pieces fall into place shortly after you've worked there for a while.

I had a job I didn't like very much and was ready to leave at the first opportunity. Shortly after I was "manifesting" a new job, I got a new boss and a new cubicle at my current job. Suddenly, this not-so-good job became the perfect job for me for the time. I put manifesting in quotes because I wasn't intentionally manifesting in the sense that we talk about it today. It was my very first job, and I didn't know anything about manifesting and stuff like that. However, the principles are the same.

Open mind

No matter what stage of the journey you are on, it's important to have an open mind. There may be things in this book you may disagree with, but it's important to see another's point of view. This is what has helped me grow and have much more success in my life. On the other hand, you may agree with everything I have to say and see the light shining above. Either way, I hope you enjoy this book.

> *Everything that man has ever built or created came from an idea—airplanes, rocket ships, government, and castles. These all came from man's intuition. These are all concrete objects created from a thought—an idea.*
> —Anonymous

Finally, I make no promises in this book. However, after reading this book, I know you will have a new appreciation for how the Law of Attraction works and how it can easily work for you.

-1-

Manifesting Marriage in 7 Days by Letting Go

I'd like to begin with how I met my wife. To me, it is the foundation of magic and everything I will say in this book.

Back in 2007, I was 37 years old and about as single as a one-dollar bill. I had no prospects. No fallbacks. No friends with benefits. No drunk dial-a-dates. Nothing. Dry as a desert.

Yes, I dated a little bit here and there. But there wasn't anything out there that looked like marriage material. My two older brothers had each gotten married and started families by the time they were 35. I was beginning to feel like the "weird uncle" who was single and didn't have any prospects. But it wasn't for lack of trying. I tried hard—extremely hard. I wished upon every star in the sky to find a woman that would be marriage material.

By marriage material, I mean she would have all the qualities I was looking for in a wife. I wanted qualities that I could live with for the next forty to fifty years because I was in it for the long haul. I didn't want this to be another failed experiment. Also, I hear about all the pain and misery of getting a divorce.

I was also looking for all the qualities I thought would be acceptable to my extended family. I know I should love and marry for myself, but I live in a world where there are other people—and they do matter. My family had high expectations. My late mother was beautiful, and the standards she had for her three boys were high. My two brothers married beautiful women (inside and out), and they made good wives—nothing to complain about there.

Unfortunately, nothing like that was coming my way.

The spender

One girl I dated for a while was lovely. She was kind and friendly. I thought maybe she could be a good candidate for the alter. However, over a short time, I found out she was a shopaholic. My bank account was not set up for that.

One day, she showed me her brand-new TV. This was before flatscreens took off, so this TV was a 48" box. It was huge. Her tiny apartment was only 900 square feet.

She told me she had paid $1,245 for the television. The following week, she was crying on the telephone, telling me she couldn't pay her rent. I told her that since she just bought a new TV, she should take it back and get her money back to pay her rent.

She was having none that. She said she couldn't part with it, so the TV was staying. If she got bounced out onto the street, so be it. As long as she had her TV, she was happy.

Since a friend had loaned me $200 many years ago when I was down and out, I offered to lend her $500 to help pay her rent. I was grateful that someone could help me in my time of need, so I felt moved to do the same for someone else. However, no less than six people (her friends and mine) told me I was crazy for lending her the money. They said that I would never see that money again.

Fortunately, I did see that money again. She paid me back. Phew! Never again. I cut the line and let her go…back into the water.

A fateful visit

At this time, I dated another woman. She was attractive and reminded me of Ellen Barkin in her younger years.

I was turned on because Ellen Barkin was a well-known actress in her day. Nancy and I dated for a while. For some reason, she was always telling me to "relax." I was relaxed. Why the hell was she always telling me to relax?

She was the youngest of nine children. This situation was too much for me to handle. I didn't want to be under the scrutiny of her eight brothers and sisters. On our final date, we had visited my brother and his family at his golf club. My brother and sister-in-law were so ecstatic that Uncle Austin had finally found someone. It was a real live person that I had been dating for more than three weeks.

The visit didn't go well at all. On the drive back, we broke up. Yes, right there in the car on the highway, we called it quits. It was about as amicable as it could get. No scratches to the eyeballs or lamps thrown across the room. It was perfect.

The bachelor

So now, I was deep in my 37th year and looking at another year of nothing. It was at this point where I stopped looking for "Ms. Right." I told myself just to stop looking. What most people do is "take a break." They say themselves that they aren't looking, but they are still looking subconsciously. This is where the magic lies. I was no longer interested in finding Ms. Right.

In my head, I had made plans to live out the rest of my life as a bachelor. I didn't play any mind games like: I will be a bachelor, but if the right one comes along, I will consider marriage. I was immersed in—and loving—the idea of being a bachelor for the rest of my life.

Previously, when I had bachelorhood thrust upon me, I felt small, weak, and unworthy. I was ashamed that I was single. I didn't want to be *Weird Uncle Austin* to my young nieces and nephews. I didn't want to be the guy who had to scrounge up some odd random date for every wedding, birthday party, funeral, or graduation that I had to attend. I didn't want to be that guy.

But now I was embracing that guy. I imagined that I would be driving around in a sports car with the top down and living life on my terms. I could get laid as often as I wanted. I could live the life of "love 'em and leave 'em." And I didn't care one bit if I showed up to a wedding, a birthday party, a funeral, or graduation with just me or some random girl I picked up the night before. I just didn't give a shit anymore.

I gave up the idea of being married, and I felt tremendous relief from my decision. I no longer stressed about the women I was dating. If they were suitable for the night, then they were good for me. I didn't have to factor in whether they were marriage material or not. The pressure was off.

The week that was

About a week after I had planned a new life for myself, I attended a ski club meeting. This ski club would sponsor weekend trips to Vermont and weeklong trips to Colorado. I was brand new to this club, and I had just joined about a week earlier. I attended this meeting with a female friend of mine. Her name was/is Chelsea, and we almost dated. However, we only ended up playing tennis together on warm summer evenings.

While at this event, I struck up a conversation with a gorgeous woman while waiting to get a beer at the beer pavilion in the meeting hall. Tina introduced herself to me and just started talking to me. I couldn't figure out why. I was new to this ski club, and I wasn't anything special. She was beautiful and had a friendly personality. "Why was she talking to me? I'm not anything special. She probably has a boyfriend—either at this event or at home. Single women that beautiful don't talk to me if they are available."

She was very friendly and talked to me regardless of me being a total stooge. She spoke about how she loved the ski club and loved taking weekend trips to Vermont. And that she signed for a few trips for January.

The conversation was pleasant. I talked to Tina up until I got my beer. After that, I said, "It was nice talking to you." And then I left. I wanted to find Chelsea and see what she was doing.

When I spotted her, she was talking to a few members of the ski club. Since she was so engaged with her friends and the conversation, I held off. I didn't want to interrupt her.

At this point, I was kind of lost. I had a beer in my hand, and I didn't know anyone at this big event. Chelsea was talking to people she knew. And then, it dawned on me, "Why the hell did I let that girl go? She was talking to me. To ME! What am I, a fucking idiot? Oh god, I've got to be the biggest fucking idiot on the planet. That hot girl was talking to me. Fuck me! I'm an idiot!"

After tearing myself apart for ten minutes, I went looking for Tina in this crowded convention hall. I spotted her talking to no less than five guys. "That slut," was my first thought. But then I realized it's just a friendly conversation. Besides, they are the ones that probably swarmed her. She was easily the most beautiful woman in that crowd, and every one of those guys wanted to be next to her.

While watching Tina talk to those five guys, I quickly realized—or assumed—that she didn't have a boyfriend in her life at this time. There is no way her boyfriend would let her talk to all those guys if he was in that room or at home. And none of those guys came close to looking like she would have dated any of them. It's not that they were unattractive; it's just that they seemed so unrefined. Also, no one's body language told me that any one of those guys could be her boyfriend.

I didn't want to be guy number six, so joining that crowd was out of the question. I stood around in eyesight, hoping she would extract herself from that group, but no such luck.

So now, I was kicking myself. "Why did I let Tina go? She was talking to me, and she was interested in all the awkward things I was saying. She even laughed at my jokes and stupid gestures. What the hell was I thinking in letting her go?"

After kicking myself and realizing I wasn't going to get a chance to talk to Tina before the night was over, I went to find Chelsea to let her know I was leaving. I decided that maybe—just maybe—I would see Tina on one of these weekend ski trips to Vermont she had mentioned. I wasn't counting any chickens, but I wasn't ruling anything out either.

Also, I was still on my quest to be the most single guy in the world. I figured that Tina wasn't the one-night-stand type, and that was the exact kind of mission I was on. I know; I'm (or at least I tried to be) a male slut. But since marriage was out of the question, I had to live the lounge lizard's life.

The magic begins

I want to stop here and explain the magic that happened here—just in case you didn't catch it. It was only a week since I made my declaration to be single. I had just met my future wife of 12 years and counting. I still can't believe how it all turned out.

Just the week before, I had let go of the idea of ever getting married. I was 37, and everyone else seemed like they were married. All my friends from high school and college were getting married and having families. I was so far from that that it kind of bummed me out. Anyway, I just let it all go.

I took the pressure off. I took my foot off the gas pedal, and I let the Universe take over. When I decided to be a bachelor, I didn't have any real plan other than riding around in a two-seat convertible wearing sunglasses.

I would just let things be as they are. To me, this is the secret that no one reveals. Yes, some do. Every good thing that had come to me came because I had stopped putting pressure on it. When I stopped thinking about it, it would finally appear. When I stopped wanting it so much, whether it was a job, a love interest, money, etc., it always came to me once I took my foot off the gas. It never failed, but I never recognized it either.

Let me remind you. I didn't "take a break." I didn't tell myself I'll be a bachelor *unless* the right one comes along. I was full in—knee-deep in cow shit—on this one. I wasn't messing around. I made a commitment--a solemn oath to be *Weird Single Uncle Austin* and fully embraced my new life.

Many authors and speakers on this subject often say you should keep your wishes and desires top of mind all day and every day until you get it. I'm not saying they are wrong. But sometimes, you have to take your foot off the gas pedal. I found this to be true in many fortunate events that have come my way. I will explain more later in the book. But for now, let's get back to the story and see how magic once again plays a role.

After I left that event that night, I stopped kicking myself. I said, "What the hell. They come, and they go." I was back on my plan of not giving a shit about who I date, when, or where. I was just going to enjoy the ride wherever it takes me. I had no plans and no prospects. I was just riding the wave.

The game

About one or two weeks later, one of the organizers of the ski club sent out an email asking members if they wanted to go to a local minor-league hockey game. At first, this had zero interest for me. Even though I played hockey in my youth, going to a minor league game just didn't appeal to me. It seemed a little cheesy. (That's my snooty attitude rearing its ugly head.)

I was about to delete the email when I remembered something that Tina had said. Even though I was dismissive of any extracurricular activities the ski club did, she told me she loved going to group events that were not ski trips. She told me she liked the picnics and the hikes that the ski club had sponsored.

After this realization, I said, "Holy shit, I bet Tina will go to this!"

The following week, I was going to the hockey game. I invited a friend (who was not part of the ski club) to come with me. He was going to be my wingman. At the arena, I got there a little early. As our group started to arrive, I somehow became a chick magnet. Three women surrounded me while I was waiting for my friend, Darryl, to show up. Also, I was waiting for Tina to show up.

This is probably the craziest part of the story for me. There was no indication that Tina would come to this hockey game. While talking to her briefly, she didn't seem to be a sports fan. However, she did say she liked extracurricular activities that the ski club sponsored.

For some reason, I still had a firm, unwavering belief that she would show up to that hockey game. My faith did not waver for one second. It wasn't a matter if she would show up; it was a matter of when and how. Would she be alone or with a friend? It didn't matter. Either way, I was going to pounce on her like an angry kitten flying out of the kitchen cupboard.

For me, this was a big deal because I did not doubt that Tina would be at that event. I would have never signed up if there was. It was not something I was interested in doing. Also, since I was very new to the ski club, I didn't know anyone. I would have felt a little awkward. I'm not an extrovert.

However, I had a firm belief she would show up. I could see it in my mind's eye. I didn't have to convince myself of this fact. It was almost as if my future self sent a message back to me telling me that Tina would show up.

Anyway, stuck between three women who seemed to want to hump my leg, I was anxiously waiting for Darryl. I was more concerned about Darryl because he was a borderline moron. He called me no less than three times to find the hockey arena. My answer was the same every time. "Take exit 15 and go straight. You will run right into the entrance." It was the most accessible place on the planet to find. Sadly, there are many Darryls in the world; therefore, many, many signs are needed—as well as friends with cell phones.

I wasn't that worried about Tina showing up. I knew she was going to show up. I had more confidence in her showing up than Darryl. It was a strange feeling and a good distraction for me to worry about Darryl. When you think about something too much, the Universe has a way of keeping it away from you. This thought didn't cross my mind. I was just conveniently distracted by Darryl's antics.

After about half an hour of standing in front of the ticket booths at the arena and pretending to be talking to these three women, I saw someone come out of the mist. It was a late October day in New England, and it can get foggy on some days. Anyway, through the fog out from the parking lot comes Tina in all her glory. I shouldn't say glory because she wasn't all that flashy that evening, but she was looking hot.

Without wasting one more minute talking to those three women, I darted over and pounced on Tina like that angry kitten.

"Hi," I said.

I didn't give her time to respond. I just reminded her that we had met a few weeks before at the ski club. She remembered me slightly. I just went on and on without giving her much time to think. I was trying to cement this little relationship before every other guy pounced on her. This situation was a live grenade. Serious action was needed.

Anyway, to make a long story short. We went on an official date three weeks later. And then another date. And then another date. And then a few more. And then, after nearly two years of these dates, we got married.

Conclusion

I tell this story because it fits in with the theme of this book. It was magic. I'm married to my dream girl. It's a fantasy. She is beautiful inside and out. She does all the cooking. She pays all the bills. She plans all the vacations. She takes care of the house and the landscaping. What do I do? Nothing. I just sit around and look pretty. Seriously. It's a good life. Okay, I give her a few backrubs every night and take out the garbage occasionally. She couldn't be happier. She tells me she loves me no less than a dozen times a day. I had manifested my dream girl.

This all came about because of magic. I had let go. I didn't play mind tricks with myself or the Universe. I honestly unequivocally let go. The Universe is smart. It knows fake "letting go." I wasn't faking it. I was on the path to be a bachelor for the rest of my life.

Secondly, I knew Tina was going to be at that hockey game. At the same time, I entertained the thought—very briefly—that if she didn't show up, how would I feel? My feeling was that I would see her somehow in the future. I didn't know how. But I knew I would see her. My feelings on that never wavered. And that is the second point. You must have absolute confidence you are getting what's coming to you.

In the coming chapters, we will explore this further and see how I manifested a job out of thin air and a house that many people would think to be impossible.

Key takeaways:

- Take the focus off what you really want
- Have patience in the process
- Trust that everything is part of a grand plan

-2-

Are Your Law of Attraction Tactics Helping or Hurting Your Success?

Many books talk about tactics and strategies for what you should do if you want to manifest good things into your life. Much of it is incredibly useful information.

Spirits in the material world?

However, a lot of it sounds like you're conjuring up some spirit by using rituals such as writing something on paper and then burning it. Or saying some chant three times or saying, "I am finished. Go now." These techniques may make some people feel good; however, many others are getting the wrong message.

That's not how this works. There is no technique for manifesting what you want. It all comes down to your belief. Some of these so-called tactics or techniques do help you believe in yourself. But that's all.

When I hear people say, "Am I doing this right?" or "I missed a day of my journaling," I get upset. I get angry because people are putting too much emphasis on the method more than who they are. The manifesting comes from who you are, not what you do. I will elaborate more on this throughout the book.

To manifest good things in your life, you must raise your vibration or frequency. This means you must have complete confidence in who you are and what you want to attract. If you only focus on tactics and strategies, you are not in a vibrational match for what you are seeking. If you are wondering if you are doing these methods correctly, then you are on the opposite end of the vibrational spectrum. In other words, you will have a real tough time manifesting what you want.

Some tools will help you manifest what you want, but there is no right or wrong way of using those tools. There is no way you can get it wrong if you believe that what you are doing is working. It's all about your belief. You must have unwavering faith in what you are manifesting in your life.

You can't do this wrong

Many people write in gratitude journals. I do. It's great to appreciate the beautiful things you have and be grateful for all the things life has to offer. This is the foundation of manifesting beautiful things in your life.

However, some people are under the belief that they could do this incorrectly. You can't. People often panic because they missed a day of doing whatever they were instructed to do. There is no need to panic because applying these methods to your manifesting is entirely optional.

People who are using these methods to manifest their dream life want specifics on exactly how these rituals or techniques should be done. They will ask, "Should I write five times a day or just three? What's better, morning or evening? When should I burn the envelope? Should I put it in a fireplace, or can I burn it over a candle?" It doesn't matter!

You aren't doing this for anyone other than yourself. You are not conjuring up some spirit in the sky. Yes, the Universe is listening, but not in the way that you think. You are writing in your gratitude journal for you—to raise *your* vibration. You are doing this for your belief system. If you believe that writing five entries in your gratitude journal is enough, then it is. If you think that writing in your journal is better in the morning, then it is.

> *"Whether you think you can, or you think you can't—you're right."*
> —Henry Ford

It's all in inside you

You are doing this. The Universe is inside you. It's not some spirit you are conjuring up from the netherworld. If you only focus on getting things right to please some god or "Universe," you will never get it right. Making this work is all about *your* belief system—not someone's rituals. Only charlatans will have you conduct some ceremony for you to get what you want.

The ritual is the belief system. You can't have confidence in what you are doing if you are only following a set of instructions. Routines and manifesting methods are good for you to get an idea of how to create a vibrational match for what you want. But it's not a rule book where rules can be applied and broken.

Like I said in the previous chapter, I manifested an opportunity to meet my future wife because of my unwavering belief that everything will happen the way I wanted them to. I didn't need any unique tactics to please some netherworld god. I had my unwavering belief, and that's all I needed.

I've manifested many other things without using any special or long roundabout rituals. But I also manifested other items by using some traditional manifesting methods. My biggest successes were when I had a total belief in what I was doing. If I had an unwavering belief in things coming to me, things would happen quickly. However, it's not that easy.

It's hard to manifest things if you don't have a firm belief that it could happen. It would be easy for you to manifest $10 if that's what you desired and believed it could happen. If that's what you wanted, you would quickly see $10 show up in your life because you thought it could.

Any plausible thing could happen in that scenario. You could get a belated rebate from a product you purchased. Sounds plausible. A relative could send you a check for your birthday. Not so far-fetched. You could find $10 next to a trash can at the beach—as I did. Actually, it was $20.

$20 for $19 sunglasses

I guess this would be a good time to tell you how I found a $20 bill while looking for a lost pair of $19 sunglasses.

My wife and I had spent a beautiful Saturday afternoon at the beach. The following day, my wife told me that she had lost her sunglasses on the beach. I told her that I would drive down to the beach and find her sunglasses. She insisted it was a fool's errand and that it wasn't worth it since they were her *cheap* $19 sunglasses, not the more expensive pair that she usually wears.

However, I was confident about finding her sunglasses because I was incredibly good at finding stuff. Let's review some of my successes before I continue the story:

Event #1

When I was fourteen, I lost my dental retainer at the beach. I had left for the day and didn't notice my retainer wasn't in my shirt pocket until I got home. Several hours later, I drove down to the beach to see if I could find my retainer. I scoured the area where I had been sitting. I didn't see anything until I saw a small glimmer of metal in the sand. There it was. I plucked it out of the sand.

Event #2

During an afternoon of ice skating on a public skating rink, my friend Tommy had fallen on the ice and broke his wristwatch. In the skating arena changing room, Tommy showed me his watch and told me that the pin for the wristband had broken off, and it was somewhere on the skating rink. I told him I would find it. He said, "Yeah, right. You will never find that thing. Look at the size of the rink and all the people skating on it." I skated over to the area where he told me he had fallen. After about a minute of staring at the ice at my feet, I found the small watch band pin.

Event #3

On a summer afternoon, I was on a beach (I love beaches) where a man asked me to help him find his lost car keys. I was sitting about twenty-five yards from him, so I wasn't sure why he thought I could help him find his lost car keys. Anyway, I walked over to where he wanted me to look. I looked in the sand for about a minute or so. Just like my dental retainer, I saw a glimmer of metal in the sand. I reached in the sand and pulled out his car keys. Seeing me with his car keys in my hand, he said, "Oh, there they are," and grabbed them out of my hand. He quickly took off to catch up with his family, who were walking back to their car.

(By the way, that guy never thanked me. I'm still having a hard time getting over that. Who doesn't thank the person that saved you from calling a tow truck?)

A critical lesson

Before I continue the story, I want to take a moment and explain how I developed my confidence in finding things. This is important to learn if you want to manifest stuff into your life. When I found my dental retainer, I could have walked home and said, "Wow, I was lucky to find my dental retainer." But I didn't. Instead, I said, "Wow, I found that retainer so deep in the sand. Damn, I'm good."

When I searched for my friend's watchband pin, I could have said, "Wow, that was lucky. I would have looked like an idiot if I didn't find that pin," Instead, I said, "I knew I would find that pin. It just took a little looking." Knowing that I felt this way—and this was the story in my head—is the real reason that I found that watch pin so quickly.

The critical thing to understand is to tell yourself a positive story and not to shrug off an extraordinary event as being lucky. Some people resent being told that they are lucky that they live in a beautiful house. They say, "No, I'm not lucky. I worked my ass for this place."

You should never shrug things off as lucky, or there was a coincidence. There is no such thing. Let's continue my story…

The quest for the lost sunglasses

Anyway, those are three events that gave me the absolute confidence that I would find my wife's sunglasses on the beach the day after she lost them. When I got to the beach, I took a quick look around the area where I remember us sitting. Nothing was found there.

I then went to the lifeguard shack to ask if there was a "lost and found" box. They showed me their little box, and the only thing in it was a lonely glove. I left the lifeguard shack and went to one of the garbage cans near the beach exit. I wanted to see if someone had placed the sunglasses on the rim of the trash can. People often do that when they find something (usually worthless) on the beach.

Right at the foot of this garbage can, I found a $20 bill. I picked it up and scanned the area to see if anyone looked like they had just dropped a $20 bill. No one seemed to be checking their pockets or walking around in circles, looking down at the sand.

I thought about bringing this $20 bill to the lifeguard shack and putting it into the lost and found box. However, I then realized how ridiculous that was. No one would think to claim it, and the lifeguards would probably spend it at the snack bar if no one had claimed the money. Therefore, I declared that twenty dollars to be mine.

After I found my treasure, I drove home. While I was happy that I found twenty dollars, I was a bit bummed that my powers of finding things didn't come through for me. When I got home, I found out why. My wife informed me that she had found her sunglasses under the seat of her car. They were never lost at the beach at all. I was relieved at this news because I realized I still had my finding-lost-stuff powers.

But it didn't explain why the Universe gave me $20 if I (or my wife) never lost a pair of $19 sunglasses in the first place. Then I realized that's not how the Universe works. It's not a tit-for-tat arrangement. The Universe is abundant. I can have a $20 bill *and* a $19 pair of sunglasses, and everything would be fine.

The biggest lesson in all of this is to have an unwavering belief in yourself and how things work. That's it. No tactics. No strategies. How do you get this unwavering belief? You develop it. There are some strategies in this book that will help you do that.

Manifesting $10

Now back to that $10, you could manifest. It would a lot easier for you to manifest $10 than it would be for you to manifest $10,000, right? It would be hard for you to believe that you could manifest $10,000 from nothing. Wouldn't you agree? That is, of course, if you are not accustomed to that kind of money. If you were a multimillionaire, then manifesting $10,000 would not seem so far-fetched.

If you are accustomed to getting a $50,000 bonus every year at your job, it wouldn't be so far out there to manifest $10,000. You would believe that it could happen. Your company could tack on an extra $10,000 to your yearly bonus. Not that big of a deal. It's only an increase of 20%. These things happen all the time, and no extra work is required.

However, if you are not accustomed to that kind of money floating around, you would do better to start small. Many spiritual teachers say it doesn't matter if you manifest $10 or $10,000. They're right, and it doesn't matter to the Universe. The Universe is abundant. But it does matter to you. How abundant do you feel right now?

Your belief system

Your belief system is the most important part of manifesting things into your life. The sad thing I see is the strict adherence to the rules of how all this works. People worry that they skipped a day of.. [whatever tactic they were using].

For instance, one manifesting tactic used a lot is to write down every day what you want to manifest. If you think that you are communicating with some outside force, you might get caught up in how to do things correctly.

However, if you believe that you are programming your subconscious mind by doing these exercises, you will not get caught up in doing things right or consistently. You would be okay if things weren't exactly how someone else would do them.

Manifesting things comes down to your belief system. You can do all the tactics in the world and follow every teacher's strategies to the letter and still fail massively. Conversely, you can play loose with the rules and have massive success. It all comes down to your level of belief.

Most of these tactics are there to reinforce your belief, not to conjure up some netherworld entity. People get caught up thinking they should please some god. You are not. You are merely raising your vibration to match what is out there in the field of potentials.

I want to illustrate something that will help you understand what I am saying about not being too strict with the rules or tactics. I'm going to introduce you to something I call a "bridge." This is a little anecdote that will bridge the gap in your understanding.

Guitar bridge

Imagine you are learning to play the guitar for the first time. If you practice a few hours every day, you will ultimately become a good guitar player. Let's say you practiced diligently every day for six months. However, during those six months, you could not practice for a few days for various reasons. Maybe you were sick, had to go on a family vacation, or your guitar string broke, and you couldn't get a new one.

It doesn't matter the reason. The point is you missed a few days of playing guitar. The question is: Would you be less good of a guitar player for missing those days? Yes, of course. Every day you didn't practice playing guitar makes you less good by one day's worth. It makes sense, right?

Now, let's look at some of the strategies people are using to manifest their desires. If you made a promise to yourself that you would write out a mantra for three months to manifest one of your deepest desires. It could be anything. It could be a new car, house, mate, job, etc. It doesn't matter.

You write out your mantra every single day. You are building up your belief that what you are going to manifest will come to you. You are programming your subconscious mind. However, there were a few days where you couldn't write out your mantra. You were sick; you were partying; you were on vacation, etc. It doesn't matter.

Now, most people who have been manifesting for some time without success would look at that scenario much differently than someone who had great success. Remember, you are programming your subconscious mind and raising your vibration. Therefore, if you skip a day, you will be one day short of what you need to raise your vibration to be.

The problem comes when you think you are pleasing some outside entity like the Universe or some nether world character. You will start to question whether skipping a day on your mantra will "ruin everything." You will begin to think that you will have to "start all over." I put those phrases in quotes because that's what I hear from people all over. They say that they had skipped a day and must "start all over."

This is not the way to think about it, and it's not the way it works. When you do these tactics like mantras, visualizations, or mind movies, you are programming your subconscious mind. You are increasing your confidence level. I hear too many people

Can the Law of Attraction Be Made Easy? | 43

asking if they are "doing it right" or "in what order" they should be doing it. It doesn't matter!

Of course, when I say it doesn't matter to people, they get confused. Therefore, I like to use the guitar bridge as a learning tool. So, let's get back to you learning to play guitar. In that same scenario, you practiced for six months every day; however, you missed a few days of practice here and there. Do you think that you "blew it" or that you must "start all over"? No. That would be ridiculous.

You wouldn't suddenly unlearn everything you learned because you missed a few days of practice. All that would have happened would be that you are a few days *not as good* as you could have been if you didn't miss those days of practice. That's it. No underworld god or Universe will take away all that you have learned because you missed a few days of guitar practice.

This is precisely how manifesting works. It revolves around your beliefs.

Diet bridge

I think many people get into this "Oh, I blew it. I have to start all over" mindset in the same way people diet to lose weight. First, let's establish the basic principle of a diet to lose weight. No matter what diet you are on, it's all about the calories. At their core, every diet has you eating fewer calories. That's how you lose weight. Quite simple.

Unfortunately, many people have many hang-ups when it comes to dieting. They try to refrain from certain food groups, and they monitor their diet every single day. The problem is when someone eats a piece of chocolate cake at the office for Barry's birthday. When that person breaks their diet, they often say, "Oh, there goes my diet today. I guess I will start on it...tomorrow!"

My question is, "Why?" Your body doesn't care about what you eat from one day to the next as long as you consume fewer calories consistently. So, if you overeat at lunch, just eat a lighter dinner. It's that simple.

I bring this up because we get caught up in this cause-and-effect thinking. Yes, you are practicing all sorts of rituals to raise your vibration and to gain confidence, but it doesn't work in a linear way. It's okay to skip a day or to mess up.

Your little mistake doesn't cancel everything out. Just like eating chocolate cake doesn't cancel out the diet. However, worrying about it and not adjusting it will disrupt the diet.

It would help if you got out of this cause-and-effect thinking. You need to have a firm belief that things will work themselves out. The Universe has your back. It's not out to get you. It won't screw you if you forgot to write in your journal or didn't meditate one day.

Conclusion

As you can see, this is a confidence issue, right? If you are confident in getting what you think about, you would have no problem getting what you think about. Unfortunately, most of us aren't on that level. There is too much linear thinking going on.

Like I said in the guitar and diet bridges, missing a day of whatever manifestation technique you are using doesn't break the spell. Sadly, most people believe this to be the case and lose confidence in manifesting things into their lives.

Therefore, focus on yourself more than some manifesting strategy. Anyone that promises that one approach works better than another is not being honest with you, or they don't know what they are talking about.

Key Takeaways:

- It's all inside you
- There are no underworld characters
- You can't mess this up
- Missing a day doesn't cancel everything out
- Your belief is the most important part

-3-

Discover the Deep-Rooted Blocks That Are Keeping You from Abundant Success

The lack of confidence in yourself and who you are will keep all your desires away from you. You need to have confidence in who you are and what you are doing. Unfortunately, like most people, you have been programmed since you were a baby to have doubts about the world you live in. Today, you are stuck with that programming—unless you change it.

Parents

Let's start with the programming you received from your parents. I could get very technical and say that you were highly malleable until the age of seven and all that other scientific stuff, but I want to keep it simple. If you want to dive deep into this, I suggest you read or watch anything by Dr. Bruce Lipton. He explains it all in a very scientific way.

However, in this book, I will give you a quick overview. Your parents programmed you based on what they knew about the world. Currently, we live in a world of perceived scarcity. In other words, if you have something, someone else won't get it. If someone else has something, you won't get it. Your parents instilled this into your head without even realizing it. In other words, they programmed you to feel lack instead of abundance.

Some parents do instill abundance, but I doubt the children of those parents are reading this book. Wealthy parents would have a much easier time programming abundance into their children. This is why children of well-to-do parents do very well in life—for the most part. Children of lower-income parents don't do as well. Therefore, the rich get richer, and the poor get poorer. Yes, education and government policies and access to certain things play a role in how people acquire wealth, but the most significant factor is the belief system installed from the day of birth.

Many hard-working parents who become somewhat wealthy through grit and hard work would probably instill a scarcity mentality into their children. They would tell their children it's all about hard work—and at any time, you could lose it all.

Wealthy parents who received their wealth by more natural means would instill a sense of abundance. They would teach their children that there is plenty of money around and yours for the taking. They would say that you only need to believe in yourself and make a few connections.

My parents were upper-middle class, but my mother was always worried that someone would sue us and take the house. If I ever got into trouble for anything, it was all about "They're gonna take the house!"

Parents can unknowingly instill a lot of fear regarding scarcity into their children. It's understandable because many families are living paycheck to paycheck. However, at some point, this model needs to end. There is much more money now than ever before. Where did it come from?

Expansion

If everything was an even exchange and you only got what someone else gave up, then money would never grow. For instance, let's say there were only $1,000 on the planet, and the economy was always about one person's gain is another person's loss. How would that $1,000 grow to be trillions of dollars that we have today? Money grows because the Universe expands.

This is what you need to understand about how all this works. Your gain doesn't mean someone else's loss. And you getting a job doesn't mean someone else doesn't get a job. They may not get *your* job, but there are plenty of jobs out there. There are plenty of new jobs created out of thin air all the time.

In some cases, when a company interviewed two fantastic candidates for one position, they decided to create a new job. That new job came out of thin air. It's all about expansion and abundance.

This is something that took me a long time to understand. I always believed there were a limited number of jobs. I would look through the classifieds or online job boards and look at the limited number of jobs. I didn't bother to question whether there could be more jobs than I was looking at or that I had the power to create a job out of thin air. More about that later.

Here's an interesting fact for those who are looking for a job. According to most job experts, many jobs (over 70%) that are available at any one time are NOT advertised anywhere. Isn't that crazy? This is precisely how I manifested the perfect job for myself. I will explain more in a later chapter, but this ideal job landed in my lap by using some manifesting techniques I will discuss later.

Regarding your parents: They instill much of what they see and experience in the world, and what they see is scarcity. What you have means someone else doesn't have. And what someone else has, you don't have. Our world would have never expanded the way it did if this scarcity model were indeed fact. It isn't.

Unfortunately, it can take years to deprogram yourself from all the damage that was done by your parents. Later in this book, I will cover some techniques I use to get beyond this damage. It's all about removing mental blocks.

School

Schools create an environment of scarcity and competition. This is one more layer of negativity that gets added to the mix. In school, there is only ONE valedictorian, and it's a winner take all mentality.

In each class, everyone is vying for that A. If everyone gets an A, what do the schools and teachers often do? They make it harder the next time, so not everyone gets an A.

So, you go through school thinking that it's all about hard work. You need to work hard to get an A. If it comes easy for you, they will make adjustments, so it's harder. This way, not everyone gets an A. It's not always like this. In college, there is usually a class for getting an easy A. Unfortunately, it isn't Calculus, Physics, or Biology. It's usually Children's Literature or some pottery class—not something that you can brag about on your resume.

The way that the schools are set up is that if you get anything less than 60%, you are considered a failure. Schools also force you to take classes for which you have no aptitude. This is why most children who come out of school lack the confidence to succeed in life. Wouldn't you agree?

I know many kids from school who were 'A' students that didn't do much with their lives. I'm not knocking them; I'm just pointing that out.

> *"The A students work for the B students. The C students run the business, and the D students dedicate the buildings."*
> —Paul Orfalea, founder of Kinko's

Obviously, this is a generalization from Orfalea; however, it does make you think.

Here's what well-known author and business executive Seth Godin had to say about getting good grades in school:

> *"The entire purpose of a good university is to give you a foundation to fail, not a foundation to get an A. And if you graduate from college with straight A's, you have to do some serious soul-searching as to why you chose to spend your time doing that."*

I'm not trying to knock people who get good grades in school; I'm just pointing out that well-known and highly educated people believe that good grades don't equate to success. It never has.

So, what am I saying here? What I'm saying is that you've been programmed to believe that good grades mean success. If that is true, then the opposite must be true: poor grades imply a failure in life.

Colonel Sanders didn't have a higher education, but he managed to be the man behind one of the most successful fast-food franchises in the world. There are plenty of people who didn't do well in school who are successful. Unfortunately, these people are seen only as outliers. The schools won't teach you about these success stories because it goes against everything they believe in—which is good grades means success in life. That would be counterproductive for the schools.

There is a correlation between good grades and success—not good grades cause success. And the reason being is that if you don't get good grades in school, you are labeled a failure. Therefore, you carry that mentality throughout your life. It's a self-fulfilling prophecy.

Children are often taught to think that mistakes are bad. Teachers mark up papers with angry red ink when children mess up. Therefore, children often fear raising their hands in class and struggle to take risks.

Social circle

Of course, all your friends and associates also live in the scarcity model. Therefore, they will program that into you on a daily or even hourly basis. It's not their fault; it's just how things are.

They are living by the same rules. They inadvertently perpetuate the idea that we live in a world where winners take all, and one person's fortune means another person's poverty.

Media

The media is continuously showboating the haves and the have-nots. Whether it's soap operas, the news, or sitcoms, there is enough material out there for you to think that some people have it better than others just by way of being born.

However, most wealthy people are self-made. Even still, the vast majority of those didn't even work that hard for it. They just got it because they had a passion for what they were doing and believed that they would succeed. They would have done it without money.

Yes, people do work hard for their wealth, but the amount of work perform doesn't necessarily equate to the amount of wealth they have.

The point is that you were programmed at a young age to believe that there are a limited number of resources (i.e., money, jobs, dates, etc.). You were programmed to believe that you must work hard to succeed. The media also perpetuates the better-grades-equals-more-success model.

I will go into more detail later about how the media can be detrimental to your ability to manifest your deepest desires. But for now, I want to cover the fact that the media has a massive effect on how you view the world and how that worldview is a view of scarcity.

Social media

Social media is no different. It might even be worse than the mainstream media because you are seeing the highlight reels of all your friends. You think they are doing great, but in reality, they are just posting the best version of themselves—just like you are doing.

So, what does this do to your confidence? It shatters it. I barely go on Facebook. When I do, I always leave feeling more like a failure. I look at all my friends and see the beautiful lives they are having. Even though I know they are only showing me and the world their highlight reel, and it isn't their real lives, I have a hard time shaking off the fact that they are doing better than me.

As you can see, I had a LOT of scarcity programming done to me as a child. It's hard to get over this stuff when it is so deeply ingrained.

As discussed earlier and will be mentioned later in the book, your ability to manifest the things you want boils down to the strength of your belief. If you don't have 100% confidence that you will receive what you ask for, you won't get it. I will share with you how to overcome this later.

Work

Nowhere is competition fiercer than it is in the workplace. You have promotions, salary increases, budget cuts, layoffs, people out to get you, etc. It's the scarcity model at its best.

As they say, it's a dog-eat-dog world. How could you possibly have any confidence in yourself while working in a toxic environment like that? It's nearly impossible to manifest a beautiful life with so much strife, competition, and negativity.

Every day that you show up to work, you are being programmed to believe that the scarcity model is the only one that exists in the Universe. Not only do we continue to fight to keep our jobs from someone younger, faster, and cheaper, but they also remind us every day who our corporate competitors are.

You hear things like:

> *The competition is going to eat us.*
> *We must kill the competition.*
> *We need to even out the competitive playing field.*

I'm not saying that competition and scarcity don't exist. Of course, every business has competitors nipping at their heels. And I'm well aware that there aren't an unlimited number of landscaping companies that can do business in a particular town.

What I am saying here is that you are constantly reminded of the scarcity model. This means that you will begin to think in those terms when it comes to manifesting money or a lover. When it comes to men, I hear many women say, "All the good ones are taken." Oh, really? I didn't meet my wife until I was

37. I'm not trying to pat myself on the back, but these women just aren't getting into the right mindset to attract the right man.

People say the same thing about jobs. I used to say the same thing about employment. However, there is an infinite number of good jobs out there. You just must focus your energy, raise your vibrations, and believe that you deserve that job. I will cover this more later.

Although you are programmed to believe in scarcity, there is a lot of abundance and expansion in the working world. Many years ago, there was only one C-level position. Now, there are many C-level positions. They create additional high-level positions all the time. C-this and C-that. Just like the Universe, businesses expand, and so do the senior positions. No longer is there just a CEO. You have "Chief" of everything else.

Conclusion

Once you are aware of the programming you had as a child, you will be more confident about who you are and what you are doing. Recognition of this programming is the first step. The next step is also to recognize that this programming doesn't mean anything. It has no bearing on your real life.

You may be following a set of programs, and you may think that it is your real life, but it is not.

So, what do you do about all this? There are strategies in this book that will help you overcome this programming. However, you need to understand that it's you that is attracting the stuff. It's not some entity that is making sure you do everything the right way. It's you that is raising your vibration to match the vibration of what you want.

Key Takeaways:

- You are a set of programs
- You were programmed since you were born
- You can overcome these programs
- Overcoming these programs is vital to manifesting

-4-

The Big Secret on How Manifesting Works

One of the more significant problems with trying to manifest things that you want is that you are too attached to the outcome. This means that if you don't get what you want, you will be disappointed. Unfortunately, this is not how to guarantee that you will have success. You must detach yourself from the outcome.

Dancing with life

An expression I have heard from several manifestation practitioners is "dancing with life." The meaning behind this saying was clear to me from the beginning; I understood exactly what they were saying.

Whenever I was in good spirits, I knew I could do no wrong. And when I knew that I could do no wrong (or didn't care), beautiful and magical things happened to me. Things just flowed my way. Chance meetings with just the right people happened more often. The influx of money occurred just when I needed it. Serendipitous moments happened, and I was always in the right place at the right time. I got parking spaces when the lot was full, or I got asked to go to the front of the line. I was just in the flow. I was dancing with life.

When I was young and more carefree than I was later in life, my friends would often say, "Everything just happens for you." I didn't think much of it at the time, but they were right. When I didn't have the pressures and worries of being an adult, I wasn't as cautious. I would often get myself into a jam, but miraculously, I would get out of it in spades.

Unfortunately, at that time, I didn't recognize it for what it was. I did understand that I was raising my vibration, and my vibration was making all those things happen to me. I kind of knew it in the back of my head—the way back. What I didn't realize was that I could intentionally make all this happen. I could deliberately raise my vibration and dance with life.

Let's cover the definition of dancing with life for some who don't grasp it. Dancing with life is having total confidence that everything is going your way. You can do no wrong. And if you do wrong, it's no big deal. If you blow an opportunity, another one is around the corner. If things do go wrong, they will soon get better. You are in utter confidence that it will all work out for you, and there is a plan for you.

You are no longer scared to do something because it might turn out bad. You no longer deliberate on matters based on the probability of success or not. You just do them.

Elon Musk

Elon Musk once said he thought that there was only a 10% probability that his company Space-X would succeed. He did it anyway.

Another time, when things were going wrong for his two companies SpaceX and Tesla, he had to make a difficult choice. He was losing money fast. He could let one company go down and put all his remaining funds into the other company. This would ensure that at least one of his companies would succeed through the hard times he was going through.

The other option was to hold on to the two companies and take a big gamble. Both could fail and leave him in financial ruin, or both could succeed. He chose to take the risk. This is someone whom I would consider dancing with life. He has the confidence that no matter what happens, it will all work out in the end.

This is the level of confidence you need daily. You can't worry if some strategy you are doing is going to work out or not. You must believe you are the creator and the source of all that comes into your life. If you sit around and worry about whether things will work out or not, you won't attract much. However, if you have confidence that it will work out no matter how bad things are, you will attract good things in your life.

Worry

It's okay to worry about some things. Of course, you will have hardships. Even Elon Musk worries about his enterprises. It's not so much about not worrying. It's more that you must have the confidence that things will work out in the end. Elon Musk has absolute belief in what he is doing even though he may have worries about his day-to-day function.

Also, it's about being okay if things don't work out. This is dancing with life. You are enjoying your life no matter where you are in your journey. You're not worrying about not having enough or never getting there. You are enjoying the ride.

Elon Musk is famous for working incredibly hard. He should. He's the CEO of three (or maybe more) multibillion-dollar companies. He is enjoying the journey. While he's goal-oriented, he's also focused on the journey. He's enjoying it and not worrying about what's going to happen in the grand scheme of things.

This is the level of vibration that most successful people have. They are enjoying the process. Obviously, there are exceptions.

I don't give a shit

When I have an "I don't give a shit" attitude, somehow everything works out for me. As discussed in an earlier chapter, I didn't give a shit about finding a wife. I let that go. I just wanted to go out and be a swinging bachelor. I was dancing with life. I could do no wrong. I didn't care if I went on a date and the girl liked me or not. I didn't care. I was going to enjoy the journey as it unfolded. As it turned out, my "bachelorhood" only lasted one week before I met my wife for the first time. This is how great dancing with life can be.

It only took a week of me being on a higher vibration to have the exact thing that I had wanted for so many years. Even while we dated, I had an "I don't give a shit" attitude. My wife later admitted to her family and mine that my "I don't give a shit attitude" was the very reason she was so attracted to me and eventually married me.

She had said that nearly every other guy that she dated acted like a puppy dog at her feet, begging and hoping she would like them. When she told me this, it made me cringe because this was precisely what I had been doing with nearly every other girl I had ever dated. I wanted girls to like me so badly that I acted like a lost puppy. I wanted a relationship so bad that I repelled people—and also made myself a little neurotic.

Finally, I just gave up on all that lovesick puppy nonsense and said, "I don't give a shit." And then, wham! My wife of 12 years walked into my life. I still kind of have that attitude. Our marriage is great, but I look at it like I'm not going to be a slave to some conformity that society has put upon me. I will love who I want and when I want. I don't give a shit if it ends tomorrow or not. I think this is healthy because neither one of us feel trapped. I believe that all things are meant to be, and there will always be another one out there.

Letting go of finding love

Another example of when letting go of finding love happened was when I was in college. From my freshman year until the second quarter of my senior year, I wanted to have a girlfriend. In my head, I was very desperate. I wanted a girlfriend for all the benefits that a girlfriend could give me—popularity, sex, love, companionship, etc.

All through the years, I had nothing. Finally, in the last semester of my senior year, I told myself to quit trying to get a girlfriend. It would be pointless. Why would I want to start a relationship in the last few months of college? When college was over, we would both go our separate ways. It would be pointless.

I decided to just focus on my studies and my friendships. I knew it would be the last semester that I would be with them before we all went our separate ways and started our adult lives.

I thoroughly washed out of my head any desire to have a girlfriend. I didn't even care for one-night stands, either. I made it a point to hang out only with my friends. Whenever we would go out drinking, I wouldn't even look at a girl. I just shut my eyes to them. I wasn't mean about it; I chose to focus on my friends and me.

As it turned out, that's not how things went. My plan to just be with my friends and not have any girlfriends went right out the window.

Since I had made my declaration of not wanting to find a girlfriend or have any kind of relations with a girl, I got more girl action in my final semester of college than all the previous seven semesters combined. I won't get into the details of my conquests, but I felt like Hugh Hefner.

Nearly every weekend, I was making a new friend with a girl—if you know what I mean. Two girls wanted a close long-term relationship with me, but I explained to them about my feelings of starting a new relationship right before we would all go our separate ways at the end of our senior year. It just wasn't something I thought would make sense. They didn't agree. They still wanted to date me exclusively. I only wished they came into my life sooner. Things would have been different.

Even though I was happy about getting the attention and affection that I had craved for all those years in college (and high school), I was also kind of pissed off. I kept asking myself,

"Where the hell were all these girls before?" I felt like I got cheated. However, I did learn something. I learned that taking the foot off the gas pedal and relieving the pressure is necessary for things to manifest.

Relax

I once dated a girl briefly who was always telling me to relax. This, of course, had the opposite effect of me relaxing. Every time she told me to relax, I would get more and more agitated.

In the end, she was right. I needed to relax more. If there is one thing that I learned in life is that I needed to relax. I was always agitated and worried all the time. And every time I relaxed and let things be at ease, things just seemed to go my way.

Whenever I'm in the grocery store and I am in a long checkout line, I get extremely agitated. I start to get frustrated with the moron who can't seem to fill out his personal check properly or the woman with the fifty coupons who insists the coupons that are out of date are still valid. When this happens, I begin to sigh, huff, and puff, and I get myself all worked up.

But as soon as I see a magazine in the checkout line and start reading it and really enjoying it, I relax. And when I relax, things start to go my way. On several occasions, the person with a fully loaded cart decided to get out of line to do more grocery shopping. On other occasions, a store manager would pull me out of the line and offer to check me out at another checkout counter where there was no line. Or I suddenly realized I had forgotten something super important and continued shopping, and when I came back, all the lines were empty.

Mellowing out and relaxing allowed me to let things go. I no longer had a tight grip. When I relax, I no longer try to control everything. Understanding this was key to being able to manifest more things intentionally.

Brain burp

Have you ever tried to remember something that should have been easy to remember, such as a person's name, where you put your car keys, etc.? However, as hard as you try, you just can't remember.

But then, you take your mind off it. It suddenly comes to you. This is you relaxing and not trying to control everything. This is a valuable lesson. Now, when I can't remember something simple such as a name, place, or date, I quickly let it go and move onto the next topic. Within minutes the thought that I had struggled to remember suddenly appears. You just must relax and let go.

Bacon and egg sandwich

Another time when letting go gave me exactly what I wanted was when I was picking up a takeout order. I had ordered a bacon and egg sandwich from a local deli, which is often packed with people waiting for their orders. I had called fifteen minutes ahead of time to place my order. This was plenty of time for them to make my sandwich and have it ready for me to pick up.

I thought I would just go in, pick up my order, and be on my way. However, when I got there, it was indeed packed with about 27 people waiting for their sandwiches. My sandwich wasn't ready, and I was a bit peeved. I asked for a coffee from the counter person and waited just like everyone else.

After about what seemed like twelve (long) minutes, I was getting a bit irritated. I then realized that I hadn't *asked* the Universe for my sandwich to be ready. I just waltzed into the deli, hoping my sandwich would be ready, and when I didn't get it, I got irritated. I was sending out some major shitty vibes. Also, before I went to get my sandwich, I knew I would be irritated if I didn't get it right away. It wasn't a conscious thought, but it was a deeper thought. And since I was irritated when I got to the deli, the thought was there even though I wasn't consciously aware of it.

Realizing that I hadn't asked the Universe for my sandwich to be ready, I took a moment and did just that. I closed my eyes for a second and asked the Universe for my sandwich to be ready. And if it wasn't ready, that's okay. I would just sit there and relax. I opened my iPhone and started reading a Kindle book that I was excited about reading. I prepared myself to wait for a long time since no one else seemed to be getting their sandwiches either. I relaxed and relished the idea that I would have a few moments to read a book that I was excited about.

As soon as I read the first sentence in that book, my sandwich was ready. I asked and then relaxed. That's all it took. I was able to relax because I was enjoying my Kindle book and my coffee.

$600 blown

When I was starting my web design company many years ago, I was contacted by a salesperson from the local Yellow Pages. This call was in the early 2000s when the Yellow Pages were still somewhat relevant but clearly on its way out.

The woman asked me if I wanted to advertise my web design business in the Yellow Pages. Knowing that no one reads the Yellow Pages anymore and that it was dying out, I said, "No, thank you."

After telling her that everything is moving to online platforms and my company was an online business, it didn't make sense to advertise in the Yellow Pages. However, she said that my printed listing would also include an online listing.

Now, she got my interest. My business was new, and I wanted to get the word out about it as quickly as possible. Therefore, having my ads also appear online appealed to me. You must remember that this long before Google Ads took off the way it is today. Facebook didn't even exist at that time.

She said the ad would be $600 for a full year in the printed book and online. I hesitated. It was a lot of money, and I didn't think anyone read the Yellow Pages anymore. She convinced me that there were still a lot of people who use the Yellow Pages. After a lot of wrangling back and forth, I gave her the go-ahead and paid $600 for the ad.

On the following day, I immediately regretted my decision. It was mostly buyers' remorse. But also, I saw the online listings for the Yellow Pages, and they were awful. And the Yellow Page listing didn't come up on search results. I felt a little cheated.

I called the salesperson on the phone to cancel my order. To make an exceptionally long story short, she said I couldn't cancel my order and that I was stuck with the ad. No refunds!

Now, I was stuck with a $600 ad in the Yellow Pages that I was very certain no one would see and/or respond to. And I was right!

For about five weeks.

After I was told that I was stuck with the ad, I just let it go. I was certain that no one would call. I just thought about how I wasted $600, and I would never see any profit from that investment.

Once I let it go and completely forgot about the ad and got on with my life, I got a call from an older woman. She sounded like she was in her sixties, and she worked at a company that needed their website revamped.

The work she needed wasn't that extensive; however, it was outside my core expertise. I told her that I wasn't sure I was the right person. She wouldn't take no for an answer. (By the way, I've had many of these clients over the years. No matter how much I tell them that I am not right for their project, they insist that I do their project.)

It wasn't exciting work either, so I quoted her a price where I thought she would just go away. I didn't want the job. It required a lot of complex web programming—which was not in my field of expertise.

Anyway, I quoted her $4,000 for the project. She said that was fine. Now, I was stuck with a project that I didn't want to do. I outsourced the project for $800 and put in about ten hours of my own time. I walked away with a nice profit.

I tell you this story because if I hadn't been okay with me blowing $600 on that Yellow Page ad, I don't think I would have gotten that project. But I was okay with it. I let it go and moved on with my life.

The funny thing is that once I got that project, I wanted more. And therefore, I kept thinking about that ad. I was essentially asking for more business. But none ever came my way.

Beginner's Luck

Have you ever tried something new and found that you were good at it the first time around? And then when you tried it again, you were awful?

I've had this experience many times. One time I was asked to play pool with some friends who were excellent at pool. I told them I wasn't good at it. They were kind and said it was not a problem. They just needed a fourth person to play. Since they didn't care if I was good or not, I didn't care either.

As we began to play, it turned out that I was good. They all commented on how good I was. The opposing team even accused me of lying about how good/bad I was. I wasn't lying. I just happened to play particularly well that day.

I've had this experience many times with playing poker, playing golf, art projects, and so on. I knew it was beginner's luck, but I couldn't explain it.

It wasn't until I dabbled in the Law of Attraction and read a lot of books on the subject that I see it for what it is. I now realize that beginner's luck happens because you are not attached to the outcome. You let things go.

You've already declared to others and the Universe that you suck [at whatever you are doing or playing]. Once that is out of the way, you can now just enjoy yourself without all the pressure of trying to be good. You are raising your vibration because there is no pressure to be good.

The disappointing part about all this is that after you have that round of beginner's luck, you start to think you are good. And then you put all this pressure on yourself to be as good as you were when you had beginner's luck. But it never works out. You have to do it the old-fashioned way—and that is practice, practice, practice.

Conclusion

If you expect to get what you hope to get, you must relax and not worry about the outcome. If you worry about the outcome, then you won't get it. It sounds like the Universe is a total jerk, but it makes sense.

You match your vibration to the level of what you want. We cover this in much more detail later in the book. If you worry about the outcome, you are vibrating at a level of lack rather than abundance. You must feel everything is okay, and there is a bigger plan for you if everything doesn't go your way.

Once you relax and just be, you will find that you will be able to manifest many more things.

Key takeaways:

- Relax, and things will come to you
- Don't be so attached to the outcome

- Relaxing allows you to match your vibration to what you want
- Beginner's luck is the Universes way of letting you know to relax

-5-

Why the Universe Gives You What You Want

Do you genuinely want to be happy, or are you just kidding yourself? I have a question for you. Suppose your level of happiness is about six on a scale of one to ten. How would you like to be ten out of ten on that happiness scale? Most people would naturally say, "Sign me up!"

Let's suppose you happened upon a magic genie who can grant you only one wish. You ask to be blissfully happy. You've agreed that you want to be 100% happy, not 60%. This Magic Genie (MG) tells you that he can make you 100% happy if you go live on a desert island, or a mountain, or a cave, or whatever. It doesn't matter where. You just need to live somewhere where there is only you.

Because, after all, true happiness is within you. People and things have an excellent way of making us unhappy. MG tells you that you don't need things to be happy. You can be 100% satisfied without anything. However, since you live in a capitalist society, you have a tough time believing you could be 100% blissfully happy living on a desert island alone.

This how I imagine your conversation with MG would go:

Magic Genie: *I can make you 100% happy. You would be happy at a level of ten out of ten. How does that sound?*

You: *That sounds great. Sign me up!*

MG: *Good. You must go live on a desert island. Loincloth is optional.*

You: *Really? I have to do that? I don't want to do that.*

MG: *Why not?*

You: *Because I don't think I would be happy there.*

MG: *You don't understand. I have the power to make you 100% blissfully happy.*

You: *Can I bring books, games, or a TV?*

MG: *Why?*

You: *I enjoy them.*

MG: *But you wouldn't need them. You would be at the pinnacle of joy. You couldn't get any happier. Nothing would make you happier. Nothing. I have the power to make you 100% happy without anything else in your life.*

You: *I know. I just think I would be awfully bored on that island all by myself.*

MG: *Maybe you're not getting this. You would be in total bliss. It would be like having an orgasm every second you were there—without all the downsides (if there are any).*

You: *I don't know. What about my friends and family? Wouldn't I need them?*

MG: *No. You would be so happy that you wouldn't need them or anything else because you are at a level ten out of ten. Why would you need anyone else or anything else if you were 100% orgasmically happy?*

You: *I don't know. It just doesn't sound like it could be so.*

MG: *You do believe that I am a Magic Genie and that I can make you blissfully happy, right?*

You: *Oh, I do believe you can grant me any wish—and even to make me blissfully happy. But I just think I would be kind of bored on that island. I would miss all my stuff.*

MG: *Isn't all that stuff an attempt to make you happier?*

You: *I guess.*

MG: *But how happy are you?*

You: *Pretty happy. I guess I'm not at a level that you are promising.*

MG: *Do you want to be at the level that I'm describing?*

You: *Not if I must live on a desert island.*

MG: *Why not?*

You: *Because I don't think I would be very happy on a desert island.*

MG [pinching his fingers]: *Ugh! I'm this close to poking you right in the eye! Listen to what I'm telling you: You would be insanely happy! You wouldn't need anything else. You would be in total bliss.*

You: *I know, but…*

And, of course, this conversation could go on forever. I hope I have made my point. Even if you were promised total blissful happiness, most of us wouldn't recognize it if we saw it. In our world view, we equate happiness with the things around us—not within us. In our capitalist society, we see happiness as having stuff. Yes, people do derive pleasure from work, family, hobbies, and things like that. But mostly, it's about the stuff we buy.

> *"I don't care about losing all the money.*
> *It's losing all the stuff."*
> —Bernadette Peters as Marie in *The Jerk*

It would be hard for us to understand that we could achieve total happiness without having all that stuff. Even if this happiness were promised to us by some magic genie, god, or anyone who had absolute power to do such a thing, we'd still balk at it.

It is time to reflect on what happiness is. What are you willing to give up to have it? Some of the happiest people on the planet are the same people who don't have a lot of stuff. They have families, social groups, daily work, and a few other things. But they don't buy a bunch of stuff to fill a void.

I say all this because many people think the Law of Attraction is all about getting stuff. This is the wrong way of looking at it.

What does this Universe want for you?

You must consider what will make us happy. If you read a lot of books about manifesting, it seems the only thing that will make us happy are cars, houses, yachts, vacations, and a bunch of other stuff. Of course, there is a sprinkling of relationships and health. But what do you really want?

Do you really want a big yacht? It takes a bunch of time, money, and effort to maintain a yacht. For what? To be happy? Why not just be instantly happy and take the boat out of the equation?

Do you really want to be rich and famous? Let's take the first one. Do you really want to be filthy rich? Do you have any hang-ups about being rich? If you're rich, you would have more cars than you can drive at one time? You would have yachts, houses, and so on. Do you really want to maintain all those things?

Of course, you would have servants, caretakers, and personal assistants do a lot of that work for you. But you still must look after *them*. You must make sure your staff is doing a good job. You are now the boss of a bunch of servants. Is this something you are ready for? Can you handle this kind of responsibility?

If not, then you will have a tough time attaining this kind of wealth. If you are not able to handle this kind of responsibility deep inside, you will not likely get these riches solely through manifesting.

It's not enough to want those things or think you want those things. You must accept total responsibility to have those things. Otherwise, the Universe won't give you those things.

The aunt and uncle bridge

I like to use the aunt and uncle analogy. For simplicity's sake, let's say you are an aunt to many nieces and nephews. You are generous with your gifts. You love to see the smiles on the faces of your young nieces and nephews. When they were young, they loved all the toys you gave them during holidays and birthdays. As they got older, you noticed they didn't enjoy the gifts so much. They were getting presents from other people. They had their own money and grew out of the whole present thing.

As time went on, you struggled to know what they would enjoy. When your nieces and nephews were young and impressionable, they loved everything you gave them. But as time marched on, it became harder and harder to please them. One particular niece was especially troublesome.

Every time you went shopping, you struggled to find the perfect gift for your niece. When you got her a gift, at first, she was happy with delight. But before too long, she brushed it aside for something else. Growing tired of performing the mental gymnastics of picking out the perfect gift, you started to pull back a little. In fact, it was so hard to find the right gift that you often sent the gifts late.

Whatever the reason for her not enjoying your gifts, you would have to ask yourself this question: *Why should I keep giving her gifts if she isn't enjoying these gifts?*

Sooner or later, you would discontinue giving her gifts. You would make rational conclusions such as "Well, she has everything she wants," or "She has grown out of it," or "She just doesn't want to feel obligated to thank me. I will let her off the hook."

Now, imagine what the Universe thinks if you didn't fully enjoy your gifts. The Universe would pull back, too. You may say, "The Universe hasn't given me any gifts, so what the hell are you talking about?"

What I'm talking about is that if the Universe knows you can't handle an 80-foot yacht, then you ain't getting no 80-foot yacht—you know what I'm talking about?

Here's another analogy I like to use to get my point across.

The rich movie producer bridge

Imagine you are a big-time movie producer. You have the power to pluck any starlet out of obscurity and make her into a top movie star, and the path she walks on glitters with gold. As it turns out, you have a niece who is quite a ham in front of the camera. She's twelve years old and likes to perform for people.

She desperately wants to be in the movies. However, you are a little hesitant. You see personality traits in her that doesn't make her suitable for being a big-time movie star. The movies are a tricky business, so you are not quite sure if you should put her in the movies.

However, she has begged and pleaded with you for the past several years to be put into one of your movies. You realize that there is a role she would be perfect for. You know she would be great in it. You have a strong sense that the movie would be great because everything you touch is gold. Your niece would be an instant movie star overnight.

However, something is gnawing at you in the back of your head. You hear what she is saying about being a movie star. But her body language is telling you something else. It's what she's *not* telling you that gives you pause.

You are very in tune with these types of things. As a big-time movie producer, you see starlets come and go. Sometimes, it isn't pretty. You are highly fine-tuned to these things. Usually, you don't give much thought to what happens to these young starlets.

But now it's your niece—your own flesh and blood. You don't want to make her life worse than it is. You know there are downsides to being a movie star—never mind an overnight success. There could be a lot of fallout if things don't go well. Her ego could be crushed; she could get in with the wrong crowd. She will give up her privacy. But you love your niece and want to give her anything she says she wants.

You meet with your niece and tell her about the movie. You ask her if this is something she wants. She says yes. You tell her that being a movie star isn't all peaches and cream. There is hard work and some hardships, and it's not all glamour. However, you still paint a pretty lovely picture because you think this will be good for her. The downsides are minimal, but ultimately, it's up to her. She loves the idea of being a big famous movie star. She wants to be in the movies, on the cover of magazines, owns a big house, and travel the world.

As she is revealing all these things to you, you start to get a thought in the back of your head that maybe she won't be able to handle all this fame so soon. You've known her for twelve years. You've known her to be a bit reserved and always needing her privacy. You also realize that she has a very addictive personality. She attaches herself to things and won't let go. On the other hand, you know that she will be just fantastic in front of the camera. Regardless of your reservations, you proceed with your plans to put her in your new movie.

Fast forward eleven months. The movie you produced is a multimillion-dollar blockbuster hit. Your niece becomes an overnight sensation, as expected. She's on all the talk shows, on every magazine cover, gets offers to do all sorts of movies at the highest rates.

Things are going great until…

Fast forward a few more years. Things are not going well for your niece. The last three movies were flops, and the producers and directors blamed her because she can't work with anyone. She constantly wants to be alone and won't listen to anyone. She would often show up on the movie set late because she was hungover from a night of binge drinking and partying with friends. She has no career, and she couldn't care less.

She's relieved that she isn't in the movies anymore. She realizes it wasn't exactly what she wanted or even what she could handle. But things are still a disaster. She is now a drugged-out, out of work, dead broke street prostitute who is trading sex for drugs and alcohol.

Your plan to make her into a world-famous movie star has ended in disaster. You saw the warning signs in the beginning. You knew deep down she couldn't handle the life of a movie star. As much as she said she wanted to be a movie star, you knew that she had specific personality traits that wouldn't make her suitable for that kind of lifestyle. Your niece said she would be happy being a movie star, but ultimately, she wasn't. Considering all this, you swear to yourself that you will never do that again for anyone—no matter how much they think they want it. From now on, you will listen to your intuition.

Now, imagine you are the Universe. Would you go around giving things to people if you knew it would end in disaster? Not likely. You want to give gifts to people that they will enjoy and can handle responsibly.

This is why it disturbs me when teachers of manifestation tell their flock to ask the Universe for everything. I came across a blog where they are telling people to play a ridiculous money manifestations game.

The billion-dollar manifestation game

The game goes like this. You write down and ask for $1,000. For every day after that, you double that amount. For instance, on the second day, you try to manifest $2,000, and on the third, $ 3,000. Do that for thirty-one days.

Do you know what that comes out to be? I'll tell you. Here's the answer: $1,073,741,824,000. That's over one trillion dollars. If you doubled $1,000 every day for 31 days, you get over one trillion dollars. Can you handle one trillion dollars? Do you think the Universe has enough cash reserves in its account to give you one trillion dollars? (It does, but can you comprehend that?)

If you can't handle it or don't believe it is possible, then it's not going to work. The only way you will manifest things is if you think you will get them. This is why I don't believe in a lot of these exercises or rituals that get thrown around blindly.

They are exercises in frustration, and they don't do anything. They are unrealistic. Magic does happen. But it must occur in the realm of possibilities that *you* believe. Start small. You can effortlessly manifest $5. That's a piece of cake.

> I did this just yesterday as an experiment. I wanted to see how long a $5 bill would show up. After reading that blog post about doing manifesting $1,000 for the 31 days, I said, "Keep it simple, people!" So, I sat in my recliner for five minutes and asked for $5.
>
> I imagined finding a $5 bill in the most unusual places. Some examples were inside a book, under a carpet, rolled up and wedged between two rocks in a stone wall, under a roof tile, in the attic, etc. What I didn't do is imagine it in all the usual places like under sofa cushions, in my pocket, in the washer or dryer, etc.
>
> I also expressed high emotions as I was manifesting. Getting $5 is not that exciting. But getting $5 when you least expect it or in a place you least expect is exciting. So, in my mind, I visualized that I found a $5 bill under a rock in the woods. (By the way, I actually hid a $5 bill in a stone wall in the woods so that someone could have that experience.) I also imagined that I was so excited that I found $5 in quarters in our attic. We had just moved into a new house, so I thought this kind of find would be interesting. Anyway, I imagined all sorts of situations, but they were situations to be excited and grateful about. That's important.

Only two hours later, I got a letter from Staples, the office superstore. On the front, it said, "Your rewards are inside." I usually quickly throw out these kinds of things because credit cards are always saying "rewards inside," which is on the condition you sign up for the credit card and spend a lot of money. Since this letter from Staples was not a credit card offer, I decided to open it.

And there it was staring me in the face: $5. I was flabbergasted. Now, I'm a big believer in the Law of Attraction—otherwise, I wouldn't have written this book—but I am still always amazed at well it works. I guess it's the unexpectedness. I would have thought these five dollars would have come in a week or so—as most things do.

Now, what I was trying to do for myself was to prove that it's so much easier to manifest $5 than it is to manifest one trillion dollars. I will cover this more in a chapter about the tactics and techniques that I use for great success.

There are hundreds of people who have made millions and billions of dollars, and they all started from humble beginnings. Some started with just a dollar. Some started at $1,000. But they all much appreciated what little they had at the time. They were grateful to make progress. They were thankful for just the small gifts.

Do you think trying to manifest millions and billions of dollars is the way to go? There are many people born into very wealthy families. They start at the top, and there really is only one way to go, and that's down. Not very many people who are born with lots of money end up growing that money in any meaningful way. They don't accomplish anything.

Would you be happy if you had a ridiculous amount of money but didn't accomplish anything? It seems empty to me. And it probably seems meaningless to the Universe as well. Think about that.

Match your vibration

Oprah once said, "You have to meet the vibration. You can't be above or below it." I love Oprah's comment because I found it to ring true.

If you ask too much, you won't get it. If you ask too little, you won't get it. Suppose you are making $50,000 a year. You tell yourself that you don't want to be too greedy, so you try to manifest a salary of $55,000 to be safe. Now, how long would you be happy with a salary of $55,000?

Now, the secret is if you were thrilled that the Universe was speaking to you—just like my $5 example—you could manifest more later.

However, there is a big difference between playing with $5 and being stuck in a job you hate and only making $5,000 more than you did before. You must appreciate what you get. If you're not going to be grateful for what you manifest—such as a meager $5,000 raise, you won't be able to manifest it. The Universe knows this.

In other words, just like Oprah said, you must match the vibration. If you ask for a billion dollars and can't imagine that lifestyle, you won't get it. If you ask for a meager pittance and won't be extremely happy, you won't get that either.

What makes you happy?

This brings me to the point of "What will make you happy? Do you know what will make you happy?" The Universe knows. You should, too.

Your happiness may not depend on 80-foot yachts and 15,000 square-foot mansions. Sadly, a lot of Law of Attraction teachers suggest doing this very thing. I know a 15,000 square foot mansion wouldn't make me happy. I would feel ridiculous in one.

Now, if I gradually moved up to that level, maybe I could handle it. If I started with a 5,000 square foot home, I could move up to a 10,000 home. Since it's just my wife and me now, I'd feel a little stupid with all those extra rooms. I would think it would be a total waste. I already believe we have too much waste in the world. If someone else wants all that, I don't have a problem with it. It's their life.

I wouldn't be able to handle that large of a house. You would have to keep all that space clean. And then you would have all the servants walking around the property. I like my privacy. I don't want the servants looking at me or walking by me.

No, a big mansion would not be my style (and the Universe knows it), so it would be counterproductive for me to manifest a 15,000 square foot mansion with servants running around talking to me and asking questions. No way. Not for me. And not for a lot of people, too.

Be clear about what you want. Many Law of Attraction teachers suggest that you go and test drive a Porsche or Ferrari. I owned an Audi at one time. To me, it was kind of fancy. I even had only my three initials for my license plate. I thought this was the cream of cool. After a while, I felt stupid in it (not to mention it broke down all the time). With my three initials on my license plate, I felt like everyone was looking at me. I hated the (perceived) attention. I soon traded it in for a Honda. That I can handle, and that is what makes me comfortable. I'm much more comfortable in a Honda.

Know your comfort zone

I have most things that I want. My demands are relatively small. I like relaxing, having success in my work, and taking vacations. Those are all things that make me happy. And those are all the things that the Universe knows that will make me happy. I'm not going to try to manifest anything that will ultimately make me uncomfortable. My Universe is my aunt and uncle, looking out for my wellbeing.

The Universe knows what's going on. I tried to manifest a tropical island cruise vacation. However, I also had anxieties about flying, and my wife hated taking any kind of cruise—too many germs or something. Guess what? The Universe said, "There are no trains to Barbados, so no can do for you, my friend."

It wasn't until I got over my anxieties about flying that I was granted a vacation to Barbados. You can't have any hesitation in what you are trying to manifest. It must make you happy, and you must be able to handle it. The Universe isn't stupid. It knows your mind better than you do.

Finally, I want to say that things don't necessarily make you happy. There are numerous studies on the correlation between having stuff and happiness. In one study, your satisfaction starts to go down once your salary goes above $75,000.

Here's a quote from CNBC:

> *"Experts say that happiness does increase with wealth, but the correlation peaks at earning $75,000 per year."*

Obviously, this doesn't apply to everyone. This is just an average. However, you need to be clear about what makes you happy. If you were told by some Law of Attraction teacher that you should take a test drive at a Porsche dealership, but deep down, you are going to feel like a total schmuck owning one, don't bother with that exercise.

If you need a new car and want to manifest one, try one more your speed. You must be comfortable with having whatever you are trying to manifest. If it makes you uncomfortable, then you are unlikely to get it. There are exceptions, but there are many people (actually most) who don't succeed with the Law of Attraction. This is one of the reasons why. They are trying to manifest things that they *think* they want, but in reality, it is not what will make them happy.

A lot of this comes from our consumer-centric culture—which we will discuss later in this book. And much of it comes from books about the Law of Attraction. You would think the authors would know this, but apparently not.

You are the Universe

Just remember the two bridges I gave you earlier. Would you give a gift to someone you know wouldn't appreciate it?

Probably not. Would you give someone a thing that would ultimately harm them? Probably not.

You are the Universe, and you are the gift giver. You just don't know it. Your mind is 95% subconscious and 5% conscious—sometimes called your ego. You know deep down what you want and what you don't want. If you try to manifest things that you think you want (based on your ego), but your subconscious is resisting, you won't get it.

If you think you want a tropical vacation, you better enjoy a tropical vacation. You can't secretly hate sitting on the beach in your bathing suit or hate saltwater. The Universe (your subconscious) knows this.

Conclusion

First, do no harm. You are the Universe. You wouldn't give yourself things that would harm you or make you feel uncomfortable doing. Yes, your ego-mind does this all the time. You eat bad food, party all night long, etc. I'm talking about your subconscious, your Universe. Your subconscious won't allow you to have things that will make you uncomfortable. And it's your subconscious that makes all the manifestation stuff work. It's not your ego. That's why the harder you try to manifest something, the more it doesn't happen. It's because you are trying to manifest things with your ego-mind.

Key takeaways:

- Recognize what real happiness is
- Know what you want
- Ask for only what's in your comfort zone

- You are the Universe

-6-

Discover the Riddle of the Abundance or Contraction Mindset

Do you have a mindset of abundance or contraction?

This is a serious question and one you seriously need to consider before you attempt to manifest anything in your life.

First, let's talk about contraction.

Contraction

What do I mean by contraction? When you are in a contraction mindset, you are in the opposite mindset of abundance. You count every penny and worry about every dollar.

Some people worry about everything. Even when we had (and still do have) money, my wife was worried about bills and money. She was a worry wort. She was a contractor. She was concerned about every penny and where it was going. Thankfully, she has now come to the other side.

You won't make any progress if you worry about money. You fear that you don't make enough. You fear that there isn't enough to go around. You fear that you aren't worthy of producing more than what you already are making.

All these worries contribute to you being in contraction mode. If you think smaller than what you want to be, you will have a tough time manifesting the bigger things that you want in your life.

Have you ever seen a hoarder's home? They have a lot of junk. They are in contraction mode. They are worried about losing every little thing. Granted, this is a severe mental problem; however, many people fall into the range of being a hoarder to being fully abundant.

The best way to overcome this fear of money and not having enough is to manage it well. The better you manage your money, the more you remove that sense of lack in your life. There are many methods of managing your money so I won't go into them here. However, I would recommend looking up T. Harv Ecker's six jar money management system.

If you worry about your bills and debts, you are in contraction mode. I'm not a money manager, but the best way to not worry about your bills and obligations is not to buy so much stuff. I know that sounds harsh, but it's really that simple.

I see so many people who worry about their finances yet have so much stuff. They have cable TV, video games, big SUVs that are gas guzzlers, and other things that they don't need. Try to find ways to reduce your expenses. Nearly every day, I am asked to sign up for a new streaming TV service. They tell me it's only $9.95 a month. These are channels I wouldn't mind having, but I know how these things add up. Therefore, I resist the urge to spend the extra money. This allows me to stay in abundance mode and afford the finer and more expensive things.

Once you reduce your spending, you will feel less worried about your bills and debts. Once you worry less about your bills and debts, you will be able to move towards a feeling of abundance without all the gimmicks that teachers of manifestation talk about. I will go into more detail in the section below.

Abundance

The problem with abundance is that people have a tough time believing that it could be true.

Universe is expanding

Here's an interesting fact. Scientists once believed that the Universe's expansion was slowing down and that it would reverse its course one day. Soon, it would start to contract to the point of a singularity.

They call this The Big Crunch. However, since the launch of the Hubble Space Telescope, many scientists are rethinking their theories. They have since discovered that the Universe is expanding at an accelerated rate. And some scientists think this will go on forever.

I bring this up because we live in a world of wins and losses—and credits and debts. We don't live in a world of unlimited abundance. The mindset is that some people have all the money, and other people have none of it. They will never get more of it because other people have all of it. However, the

Universe is expanding. The Universe is making new stars, galaxies, and planets out of nothing!

This is the mindset you need to adopt. Money is made from nothing. If you want to look at the world economy and how money is made from nothing, I suggest you go to YouTube and type in: *How The Economic Machine Works in 30 minutes by Ray Dalio*. Ray Dalio is one of the wealthiest fund managers in America. In this video on YouTube, he talks about how credit is created out of nothing. And that credit is money. Money is made from nothing.

This planet was made from nothing. The world's population was created from nothing. The problem is we don't see it that way; we see it as an exchange. Cars are made from raw materials like iron and steel. Therefore, there was an exchange of materials from one form to another. This is finite, but money doesn't work like that. Money is infinite. You must believe that it is.

My experiment

Here's an experiment I created for myself. I was going through a tough time in my life many years ago. I wanted to feel abundant, but it was hard for me to conjure up that feeling. So, I decided I would go down to the bank to get 100 $5 bills. My plan was to tip every person I possibly could with either $5 they usually wouldn't receive or an extra $5 on top of the 20% tip I usually tip.

When I first cashed the check, the clerk initially gave me 5 $100 bills. No, I told her I need 100 $5 bills. She must have thought I was going to a strip club or something.

Anyway, when I walked out of that bank with $500 in cash, I was feeling abundant and…

I need to back up from this story a little bit because something incredible happened, and this is the most appropriate time to tell you this.

A few days before going to the bank and cashing a check, I sat in my recliner and formulated this plan. I planned on going to the bank and cashing a check for $500. Two days after I had formulated this plan, I got a check for $6,700. This was totally unexpected. This was from an investment I had many years earlier, but it was unexpected.

As soon as I got that surprise check, I knew the Universe was speaking to me. There was no other choice but to follow through with my plan. I immediately went down to the bank. I asked for $500 cash and deposited the rest of the check.

My plan was going to give $5 tips to everyone I possibly could. This was for every counter person, valet, grocery store bagger, carwash personnel, etc. An extra $5 would go to my hairdresser, waiter, bartender, etc., on top of the normal tips I usually gave to those people. This was my way of feeling abundant.

My feeling of abundance came from the fact that the money was already spent. I was already going to give the money to people, so the money wasn't mine. In my mind, the money was already out the door.

I kept the money in an envelope and promised myself that it was only to be used for tips. I always made sure to keep around three $5 bills in my wallet. This money was separate from all the other money in my wallet.

The rule was that those $5 bills could not be spent in any way other than for tipping someone. If I were short on cash at Starbucks, then I would use my credit card (which I usually don't do) and throw $5 into the tip jar. I would leave the remaining two $5 bills alone. Those were reserved for tips only. I wasn't allowed to pillage the tip money for other expenses, even if it was an emergency. I had a credit card for that.

Knowing that I had all the cash sitting in an envelope and earmarked for tips gave me a real sense of abundance. I don't think I could have conjured up that feeling on my own. As discussed in a previous chapter, some Law of Attraction teachers suggest going to a Porsche dealership and test driving a Porsche. If you have an old clunker, this might be a very awkward situation for you.

Anyway, this was my version of not only feeling abundant but being abundant. So, I planned to give away this money for the next few months. I figured it wouldn't take that long. I was a regular at Starbucks, Dunkin' Donuts, and many local eateries with tip jars. And at the sushi bar, I would throw in three $5 bills. I was throwing money everywhere. After all, in my mind, the money was already spent. As soon as I cashed out $500 from that check, the money was already spent.

So off I went. I tipped every counter person that had a tip jar. I even tipped some people who didn't have a tip jar. I tipped grocery baggers; I tipped the junk removers; I tipped the maids extra. Unfortunately, after tipping counter people and grocery baggers, I ran out of people to tip $5.

Since there were only a few places I visited regularly, I was having a tough time burning through the $500 I had designated for tipping. Also, it started to become quite awkward for the counter people and me.

At first, they were happy to get a $5 tip when most people would throw in a $1 bill. They thought maybe I was making up for all the times I didn't tip. However, week after week, and sometimes every day, I would throw in $5 into the tip jar, the counter people started to look at me funny. They felt like maybe I was buying them off, or I was asking for a special favor. I wasn't. I was just trying to be abundant.

Even the grocery baggers refused my money. Needless to say, my abundance experiment didn't last as long as I had hoped. After I burned through only a $125 of $5 bills, I put a pause on the abundance experiment. Some people can do this abundance without feeling bad about it. Not me. I was too self-conscious.

My father would throw $20 bills into people's faces without any problems. (Unfortunately, I inherited my mother's neuroses.) The valets, the motel maids, anyone who looked like a good candidate for $20 would get a $20 from my father. My father would see maids in the hall of a motel and give them each $20. They weren't even cleaning his room, but he would give them each $20 for the hell of it. The valets loved him. He would get us the best (and usually unavailable) seats in a crowded restaurant by slipping a $20 bill or two. He was able to pull it off.

Giving out $5 tips to people I would never see again would be a lot easier. The problem for me is that I had visited the same places over and over. After a while, it didn't feel like abundance; it felt like an expectation. The merchants didn't do anything wrong. For the most part, they appreciated my gracious tips.

However, I was still feeling a bit awkward. I know it was all in my head, but it was hard to overcome.

I couldn't sustain the pressure of feeling awkward. This is why I say that you need to feel confident in what you are doing. If you go to look at million-dollar homes but don't feel comfortable, you will be hampering your manifestation.

Now, I understand the concept behind the process, which is to get comfortable with it. However, going from a $350,000 home to a multimillion-dollar home is a big step, and it would take a lot to get comfortable with. A lot of people like to tell you to do this, but I know a few people who did this and said it was a disaster. They felt uncomfortable, and it didn't do anything to keep their faith in the Law of Attraction.

Fake abundance

This is where you think you are abundant but are not. This means you have debt on credit cards and a mortgage on a home. You may feel rich and abundant on the outside; however, on the inside, deep in your subconscious, you know that if you lost your job or other regular income, you could be out on the streets.

This isn't feeling abundant. Being abundant means that you could lose all that you own, and everything will be fine. This is why the rich get richer. They feel superabundant. They have so much money in the bank that if their house burned to the ground with all the furnishings and the yacht sank, they know they would be okay. They don't worry about it.

The worst thing about having a nice car is worrying about it. Being abundant means having a nice car where you can replace it in a heartbeat should anything happen to it. Do you feel that way with your car now? What about a beach chair? Would you worry that you wouldn't be able to replace a beach chair? No. That's the level of abundance you need to feel about an expensive car.

I paid cash for my Honda. I also paid cash for my home (which I manifested. The story in a later chapter). I have nothing to worry about in terms of debt. I have insurance on both. That wasn't always the case. I had debt, but I was feeling like a big shot with credit cards and beautiful cars. But I didn't own any of it. It could all be taken away from me.

To feel abundant, you must feel real abundance. The mistake I made with my $5 tip experiment is that I started too high. I should have just started with $1 or $2. I don't always tip counter people. Sometimes I don't have any one-dollar bills, and sometimes I don't get outstanding service. However, I should have done the same experiment with $1 or $2 and made a commitment to do that. This way, no one would feel awkward. They wouldn't feel uncomfortable about me tipping them every day, and I wouldn't feel embarrassed that they were feeling awkward and that I wasn't as rich as maybe a $5 tipped warranted.

I've seen too many failures where people try to run before they could crawl. I have some strategies later in the book that work well in this department.

Find your comfort zone

I'm very much an introvert. I don't like my face plastered all over the place, and I don't like taking credit for things I've done. I don't want a lot of attention. So fancy cars, big houses, and elegant jewelry just don't suit me. Unfortunately, it took me a long time to realize this. I was buying into what other people would think would make me happy.

It is for this reason why I like to give to charities anonymously if I can. Unfortunately, it doesn't always work out that way. I had once given money to *Smile Train*. They are a charity that helps children repair their cleft palate. Sadly, these children don't get these repaired until they are in their early teens. In America, this is done at an earlier age before the child is aware there is a facial deformity. Anyway, I had given them lots of money over the years. After my first donation, they sent me the profile of one of the children that my money helped.

Unlike most people who would feel a sense of pride and joy and would want to read more about the child they helped. I didn't. I was actually furious that they sent me this material. I even wrote them an angry letter to tell them not to send me anything like that again.

I was indeed crazy. I don't know what it is. I like helping, but I just feel awkward about getting the credit. I feel like I'm too much in the spotlight. I guess something happened in my childhood that I can't let go of.

Anyway, I didn't donate again to that charity for about a year. But after a year, I continued to donate to them because it gave me a sense of abundance—even though I could have used that money myself. I finally got over my aversion to seeing the people that I've helped. I don't exactly look at their new smiling faces with pride, but I don't write angry letters either.

Conclusion

The point in all of this is that you need to find your comfort zone when it comes to feeling abundant. If it makes you uncomfortable, then find something else.

Hiding money in the woods and donating anonymously to charities works best for me. I'm not a big showy person. You need to do what's comfortable for you. Yes, you can stretch your comfort zone, but it's not likely you will become a completely different person. You should acknowledge that while you are on your manifestation journey.

As I said in a previous chapter, you need to be 100% confident in what you are doing--whether it's feeling abundant or asking the Universe for something you want. It's pretty much the same thing. Feeling abundant is asking the Universe for stuff.

Key takeaways:

- Worrying about money is a contraction mindset
- Move away from contraction and toward abundance
- You must be comfortable with feeling abundant
- Fake abundance and feeling uncomfortable will thwart your success

-7-

If Positive Thinking Hasn't Worked for You, Read This

Many people perpetuate the idea that positive thinking is paramount to the success of manifesting stuff that you want. I'm not against the idea. However, I believe that visualizing a rosy picture won't exactly get you a rosy picture.

I do believe that being positive does work. But there is a big difference between *being* positive and *thinking* positive. Thinking positive is a chore. Being positive is not. However, you must think positively before being positive.

For certain situations, I believe that thinking of the worst-case scenario can work in your favor. I'm willing to bet that the worst experience you've ever had was one that blindsided you. It came out of nowhere. Maybe you were on vacation, and you got a deadly bug bite. Or you were picnicking, and some tragedy occurred. I don't want to get too detailed because many of these events can be quite horrific.

However, what I want to get across is that you never expected them. You didn't foresee any of these unfortunate events. You were oblivious to the world, and you didn't have a foreboding feeling of any tragic event happening.

Unexpected disaster

When I chipped my two front teeth in college, I didn't foresee that coming. I was too busy living in a rosy world.

I was in college and on my way to go to the homecoming dance with my date. I was a freshman and excited by all the newfound freedoms I had. I drank a little and smoked a little marijuana. In my world, nothing could go wrong—except for that sprinkler in the middle of the yard. I tripped over it and smacked my face on the street curb—nothing to break my fall other than my chin and my nose. My forehead was no help to me at all. When I got up, I felt like Bobby Clarke from the Philadelphia Flyers hockey team. Just bits of front teeth. My happy and blissful evening was shattered.

You probably have similar stories.

By the way, I had visualized how that evening was supposed to go. I imagined I was going to have a lovely evening with my date. I did all the positive visualization we've been taught over the years. But it didn't happen that way. I didn't have a lovely time with my date at the homecoming dance. What I got were two chipped teeth.

I learned over the years—and through trial and error—that doing the opposite might have done me some good. Maybe.

Sometimes we want something so badly that our emotions and state of being are dependent on the outcome. This ties up our thinking. And the Universe has a funny way of showing you the reality of how all this works. I will give you a few examples of what I mean.

New job

For many years I was looking for a new job. I had been out of work for a while, so I was getting desperate to land a new job. I was sending out some bad vibrations because of my desperation. However, I did get a few phone interviews, but most of them didn't go anywhere.

Usually, when I got a call about a phone interview, I was happy yet incredibly nervous. I imagined all sorts of worst-case scenarios, such as I would be sweaty during the phone interview. Or they would call me out on something that I put in my resume. I wouldn't have the right answer, and so on.

To my surprise, most of these phone interviews went very well despite my nervousness and worst-case scenarios firing off in my head. Some of these opportunities didn't go further than the phone interview. Many were not a fit for me, so I didn't follow up. However, on a few of these phone interviews, I was asked to come in for an in-person interview. Two of these job opportunities I remember particularly well. They both ended in a complete disaster.

Job interview I

The first in-person interview I had was soon after I finished a phone interview with a high-level manager. He liked me a lot. He had a lot of great things to say about my resume. He liked what I had to say during our conversation on the phone. He had all sorts of praises about my background and how I was answering his questions. Since he was the one who was going to make the final decision to hire me, I was happy that I made a strong impression upon him. However, I still had to meet with one of his subordinates at their office. That was fine with me. I had his full endorsement. How hard could this be?

Before my interview, I started to practice some positive mental imagery. I did all the shit gurus tell you to do. I looked myself in the mirror and said, "You're good enough; you're smart enough, and doggone it, people like you." In all seriousness, I stood in the mirror and repeated many of the positive affirmations that the gurus tell you to do. I also posed like Superman for several minutes at a time.

In the evening, I would lay on my bed for ten minutes and visualize how I was going to make a great impression at the interview. I rehearsed in my mind how well the conversation was going to go. I imagined the manager calling me up and saying, "Wow, you made quite an impression on Lisa. When can you start? And by the way, I'd like to give you an extra $10,000—if that's okay with you." I imagined Lisa posting on Linked In about her experience with our interview and telling everyone that I was a model interviewee.

After doing these positive affirmations and visualizations, I went to the interview to meet with Lisa, the manager's direct subordinate. Starting with the handshake in the lobby, my experience with Lisa was a total disaster.

After the disappointing handshake, I followed Lisa into the conference room. Within the first few minutes, she was tearing apart my resume, figuratively speaking. She asked about every minute detail in it. No answer was good enough for her. She kept pounding away at the questions, the comments, and the follow-up questions.

I felt like I was on the defensive all the way. I even reminded her in a very delicate way how much Greg—the senior manager I had the phone interview with—loved me. Lisa was not amused. The interview lasted about 22 minutes—twenty-two minutes too long.

The recruiter who set up the interviews called me and asked me how it went. I told him it was a disaster of epic proportions and that I would never work with that woman in a million years.

Job interview II

This next story is equally bad, especially since I followed all the conventional wisdom out there—for both job searching and positive visualizations.

I had a great phone interview with Stephanie on the phone. She would be my direct report. She liked me and wanted to bring me in for an in-person interview. The plan was to meet the rest of her team—about six other people. That sounded good to me.

I put on my positive visualization cap. At the advice of some job guru, I created a mini-presentation to give to the group. I liked the idea. I figured it would take the pressure off me, and I could dictate how the interview would go. The presentation was about five pages long, with a nice sprinkling of images and charts. It demonstrated that I was competent in the role that I was interviewing for. I made eight copies of this presentation. It set me back about $80, but I wanted to make a great impression, so I figured the expense was worth it. I wanted to knock this interview out of the park.

With my presentation finished, I visualized how the whole interview would go. It went something like this. All eight of us are sitting around a typical conference room table. They ask me a few questions that I answer with ease. Then during one of the questions, I would say, "It's funny you should ask me that. I have this presentation that will answer that question." I would pass around my presentation to everyone.

Then I would hear their feedback:

> "Wow, you are a genius."
> "This is good. How did you come up with this?"
> "You did all this by yourself? Great work."
> "This is really forward-thinking."
> "This is brilliant. I've never seen anything like this."

And about fifty other massively impressive compliments that I could visualize. I then imagined all of them shaking my hand as I was leaving. I envisioned Stephanie calling me up and saying, "Wow, you knocked it out of the park. They love you. Can you start in two weeks? I know you're not working right now, but this will give you time to goof off and do whatever you want before you start your new job. And I hope you don't mind, but we'd like to bump up your salary by $10,000 if that's okay with you."

I visualized that scenario over and over for five days before my interview. I was so solid on this positive visualization that it was coming out of my ass.

On the day of the interview, I met with Stephanie in the lobby. They were doing some construction in the lobby, so there were no desks or chairs to sit. I had to stand awkwardly and wait for Stephanie to come and get me. Fortunately, it was only a few minutes of standing awkwardly.

After a nice handshake, we walked back to her office. She sat me down at a small café table that seats three people comfortably—but no more. It was just her and me. I began to wonder how six other people were going to sit at this small little café table. Then she told me it would be just her and me.

This news immediately threw me off my game. I had my briefcase filled with eight presentations ready to pass around to the group. Now, I would only be presenting to one person. I felt awkward, especially since my presentation was explicitly designed to be given to a group. I kept it in my briefcase until the right moment.

Stephanie asked me many challenging questions as if she were interviewing me for a position with the CIA or Goldman Sachs. I felt like a goalie defending pucks everywhere. I kept thinking about the presentation in my briefcase. There didn't seem to be a moment where whipping out the presentation would be appropriate. It made me feel awkward to have a whole presentation for one other person. The whole scene was not going as planned. Nothing in my visualizations rang true. The interview was a complete disaster.

Finally, the interview was over. I never presented my presentation. On the one hand, I felt it would have been a smart thing to do, but on the other hand, it would have seemed very awkward. I had not visualized presenting to one person.

This interview was a disaster, but it shouldn't have been. The person who interviewed me in person was the same person who interviewed me on the phone. It should have been a done deal. I wasn't overconfident, and I knew that I had my work cut out for me. It's just that the reality didn't match up to my visualizations, and it threw me off big time.

Job interview III

After those two disasters, I had read more books about magic and the Law of Attraction. One author had mentioned that wanting something too much will keep those things away. It's all that "lack" stuff. Anyway, one thing she suggested was to think of the worst-case scenario to keep your wanting at bay. Think of the worst-case scenario and be okay with it.

Soon, I had an opportunity to put that into practice. I was interviewing for a copywriting position at a small advertising agency. I was brought in to meet with the president of the agency and the creative director. Instead of thinking about how I was going to make a big splash and all that other positive shit, I only thought about the worst-case scenario.

I imagined the two interviewing me and asking me the most difficult questions I could come up with in my visualizations. I imagined myself sweating profusely and wiping my brow endlessly. I imagined that the room was unusually hot, but I was the only one who felt that way. I imagined them asking me why I was sweating so badly.

I then ratcheted it up a notch. I imagined that I threw up all over the conference table. I then imagined that I got super defensive and walked out on the interview in shame. I had to tell my wife that I blew the interview. My wife and I were getting in a big fight—her talking about financial ruin. We're now out on the streets selling pencils out of tin cups. I was really going for it in my worst-case scenario visualization.

The reality

When I got to the interview, they greeted me warmly. The president and creative director walked me into the conference room. The president, Dave, asked me a few easy questions. Of course, I had the "Tell me about yourself" question, but the way Dave phrased it, the answer flowed out of me effortlessly. In other interviews, I had great difficulty with that question, no matter how prepared I was. The creative director also asked me a few good questions that allowed me to express myself without feeling nervous or awkward.

Basically, the interview was a conversation between three people rather than an interview. I felt so comfortable. When I left, I remember having a wonderful feeling. I even felt that if I didn't get the job, I was so proud of myself for putting on a flawless interview.

I told my wife that there was not one thing that I regretted in that interview. I didn't regret one answer, and I didn't regret one gesture. I didn't regret asking too many questions or asking too few. I had no regrets—no second guesses. I was so proud of the performance. I didn't care if I got the job. I told myself that if I could do that with every other interview, I would have a new job in a matter of weeks.

Two days later, they called me and wanted to hire me.

That, to me, was the power of the worst-case scenario visualization technique. I have so many examples of that working for me; it's unbelievable.

Under pressure

Here's one more example of how thinking of the worst-case scenario can bring about positive results.

I was working at a company where I had to put together a big presentation for the following day. I had been working on it for a week, but the final was due the next day. My boss had been looking over my shoulder all week. He was getting nervous about how I was doing with this project.

He wasn't happy with my progress, and I didn't blame him. It was awful. I struggled with putting this whole thing together. I worked until 10:00 pm trying to figure out how this whole thing should come together.

Just as I was ready to give up and go home, something clicked. I immediately saw how this whole presentation was going to come together. I worked for the next three hours to finish the entire presentation. At 1:00 am, I went home.

The next day, my boss came in telling me how he was having a conversation with me last night. I knew what he meant about "having a conversation" with me. He only imagined a conversation with me. He told me how he was arguing with me about the project. He was tossing and turning all night long, thinking about me and this awful presentation. He said he was upset that he would have to call the client and give them the bad news about the presentation.

Finally, after he ranted for a while, he asked to see the presentation. When he looked at my computer screen, his eyes opened wide with a glow, and then a smile came across his face. "Wow, this is fantastic," he said. "I will send this to them right away." He then looked at me and said, "You had me worried there. I was up all night."

Looking back, I see that my boss had the worst-case scenario planted nicely in his head. He imagined all the worst-case scenarios. He would have to go to the client with the bad news.

Crabbie's beer

The worst-case scenario has worked for me on so many occasions. I even use it on not-so-important stuff. One time, I used it to get one of my favorite brands of beer. A liquor store that was close to me was usually out of Crabbie's—that's the beer I wanted.

Often, I would have to go across town to get it. On a few occasions, I imagined the worst-case scenario before driving to the liquor store near me. I imagined they didn't have enough in stock and that the store owner was rude. I imagined I would be arrested for inquiring about getting Crabbie's at the liquor store. I imagined that I found a bunch of Crabbie's, but then I left my wallet at home. Upon my return to the liquor store, all the Crabbie's were gone. The liquor store owner would laugh in my face while some snot-nosed kid pulled down my pants. I imagined all sorts of crazy scenarios.

By the way, all this visualization only took a few seconds on my way to the liquor store.

So, let me clarify some things. This worst-case scenario doesn't mean you look at life with a dark shadow over your head. This strategy, method, formula, or whatever you want to call it works for an event or something you want desperately to turn out in your favor. This is why I think it works so great for job interviews.

The real secret to the formula

There is a second part of the formula that I need to clarify if I haven't already done so. You must be okay with the outcome. You must be okay with things not turning out the way you had initially wanted them to.

For instance, for the job that I got where I visualized that I threw up all over the conference table, I imagined that I was okay with the outcome of totally blowing the interview. I envisioned that it wasn't the right job for me. I visualized that if my wife divorced me, I was a free man, and I could live the bachelor life (don't tell my wife that!).

I visualized that if I was destitute and selling pencils that it was just what I needed. I needed to get back to my roots and start anew. First, I would be a sidewalk pencils salesman, then move up to street umbrellas, and then finally Lamborghinis. I was okay with all the disastrous outcomes. This is how it works.

Creating a worst-case scenario allows you to get out of the lack mindset. If you want something too badly, you won't get it. With this formula, you still want it, but you are okay with whatever outcome you get.

You may have heard of the phrase "Hope for the best and plan for the worst." This is a good phrase, but most people don't fully visualize the "plan for the worst" art. They just gloss over it. They may have a few ideas floating around in the back of their heads. But they are not diving deep into the visualization part.

You may have heard the instructions for public speaking is to imagine the audience in their underwear. This visualization doesn't go far enough. So, what if you imagine everyone in their underwear? What does that really accomplish?

How about imagining yourself giving a speech to the local women's business group. And then, some snot-nosed kid pulls down your pants. The women are laughing at your tiny, tiny, super very tiny penis. They are laughing hysterically and pointing at you. They are making comments like, "Look, it's an acorn on a bean bag!" And then you run off stage with your pants around your ankles. However, you trip and fall. Now all the women are laughing at you with your shiny fat ass sticking out high in the air. And then that snot-nosed kid takes a Super Soaker shoots water right up your ass.

Finally, you go home in shame. You can't face anyone ever again. But in the end, you are okay with how things turn out—believe it or not. Maybe, you discover something about yourself that you wouldn't have discovered if you hadn't shown your willy to fifty women at the town civic center.

Now, after that visualization, you will have no problem giving the best speech in the world. You would have prepared for the worst.

Do you see how this works? I use it all the time for parking spaces, lines, etc. Remember, you are asking the Universe for what you want, but you are removing your emotions from the outcome. For example, if you want a sweet parking spot in front of the grocery store, think that thought. But then imagine that not only every parking space is filled, but the closest parking spot is half a mile away.

I can't tell you how many times this has worked for me.

Look, I'm not against positive visualizations. However, when you keep visualizing, you are essentially asking. Don't keep asking. Set yourself up to receive. When you stop asking, then you are ready to receive. Take your deep desire off the table.

Here's the Formula:

Step 1: Ask for what you want (parking space, successful job interview, etc.)

Step 2: Visualize the worst-case scenario (crowded parking lot, throwing up on the table)

Step 3: Be okay with the result of your worst-case scenario (it will all work out in the end)

The beach ☹

Okay, since you asked for it. Here's another time where positive visualization was a total disaster for me. This is so painful; I'm not sure I can share it—even 40 years after it happened. But here we go.

I was on a beach sitting by myself. I was fifteen at the time. I saw two very hot blondes sitting on their beach towels about twenty-five yards from me. I was checking them out as discretely as possible. They were checking me out—or so I thought. My imagination tended to go wild in my early teens.

I sat there, trying to figure out how to approach them and introduce myself to them. I came up with all sorts of scenarios in my head of how to contact them. None of my ideas appealed to me. Finally, I decided I would buy the two of them drinks from the snack bar. What I mean by drinks, I mean lemonades, not margaritas. I was only fifteen at the time.

Once I decided to get them drinks, I had the whole thing visualized in my head. I imagined bringing them the lemonades. They would thank me for the drinks. They would invite me to sit on their towels next to them. They would get into deep conversation with me and laugh at all my funny jokes. They would tell me how cute I was with my dimples (on my cheeks). They would fight over who could rub lotion all over my body.

Okay, that last one was a bit of a stretch. I think I may have reined it in a little bit. Anyway, I imagined that I was the guy—the guy who had it all. I had the body, the dimples, the sense of humor, the lemonade. I had it all, and the two blondes lapped it up like two lost golden retriever puppies. It was a beautiful visualization. Nothing could go wrong.

However, I was still a little hesitant. Maybe, something could go wrong. It was natural to feel that way. After thinking about it, I decided not to think about what would go wrong for fear that it might happen. I wanted to keep things positive. After all, positive affirmations and visualizations work, right?

So, the moment of truth came. I walked up to the snack bar and ordered three lemonades. They served them in white Styrofoam cups and placed them in a cardboard drink tray. With the tray in my hand, I walked bravely to the beautiful young blondes (actually, they seemed to be a bit older). I asked them if they would like a nice cold drink.

"No."

"No."

"No?" I asked, wondering why anyone would refuse lemonade from a nice guy like me. Who the hell doesn't like lemonade!

"No."

"No."

"Okay. But these drinks are awfully refreshing and delicious."

Actually, I didn't say that last line. I just said that in my head as I walked away in humiliation and embarrassment.

What I neglected to find out before I created my plan was to see if they even spoke English. My town was a popular destination for summer tourists from Europe.

Anyway, they sounded like they were from Sweden…and not thirsty one bit! They apparently didn't fully understand me or put on quite a performance. I walked back in shame with three lemonades in a cardboard drink holder. What was I going to do with three fucking lemonades!

Ugh! I was mortified.

It was indeed awful. I can't even tell you the rest of the story because it's just too painful—even after all these years.

Looking at this situation again today, nearly forty years later, I should have used the worst-case scenario formula. If I had known about it, I would have visualized that the two girls were spitting in my face, pulling down my bathing suit, and laughing at my wiener.

I would have imagined that I dropped the lemonades and ran for the dunes. As I ran for the dunes, I would trip over my feet and fall on my face because my bathing suit would be around my ankles. And then a snot-nosed kid would fire a Super Soaker right up my ass and say, "Ha-ha!"

Of course, I would be okay with this worst-case scenario. Although it is hard to see an upside to this horrible scenario, I would come up with something. I'm not sure what that would be at the moment. Anyway, armed with this worst-case scenario, I am confident that the scene wouldn't have turned out the way it did.

Manifesting a negotiation

When my wife and I purchased our home, we had a home inspector look at the house. In the report, several repairs were needed to make the home livable. Some of these included fixing a chimney, repairing portions of several roofs, and carpentry work on outdoor patios and porches.

We had already made an offer, and it was accepted. However, upon seeing the inspector's report, we felt we needed a reduction in the offered price. After looking at the total amount of repairs required for the house to be safe and livable, we asked the seller for a $25,000 credit (a reduction in the original offered price).

Through our real estate agent, our request for this credit was sent to the seller. We waited for a reply. There were three basic scenarios:

1. The seller accepts our request in full (Yay!)
2. The seller refuses our request (Boo!)
3. The seller splits the difference with a $12,500 credit (Meh.)

As we were waiting for a reply from the seller, I thought about the three scenarios or outcomes. Scenario #1 wouldn't be a worst-case scenario because we got what we wanted. However, scenario number two was also not a worst-case scenario.

The way I looked at scenario #2 was if the seller flat out refused our request for a credit, then it would be easy to walk away from the deal. I figured the seller wasn't reasonable. I would have taken it as a sign this house wasn't meant for us. We were destined to find another more suitable home.

To me, the third scenario was easily the worst-case scenario. If we got half of what we asked for, it would have been harder to walk away from the deal. And since it wasn't what we wanted, we wouldn't have been thrilled. Splitting the difference never satisfies anyone.

Also, I know my wife would have accepted the offer from the seller. She loved the house much more than I did. I loved the house, but not enough where I couldn't walk away from it. I knew my wife would accept the deal but ultimately would not be happy about it.

Knowing all this, I sat down quietly on my sofa and focused on the worst-case scenario. I imagined that my wife was willing to accept a credit in an amount that was less than $25,000. I imagined that I disagreed and that we should hold out until we got the full credit amount—even if it meant walking away from the deal. We would get in a big fight.

My wife would forever blame me for losing her dream home. I imagined all my relatives and family members being furious with me for not being reasonable. On and on it went with this worst-case scenario. Then at the end of my visualization, I asked myself if I was okay with the result of this worst-case scenario.

The answer was a resounding yes. I felt that losing the house may seem bad at first, but ultimately, we would recognize that it was not the house for us. It was way too big for us, and it needed more repairs than we wanted to invest in—both in time and money. Therefore, I was very much okay with this worst-case scenario.

The following day, our agent submitted our request to the seller. We got a reply, and the seller said yes to our request. We got the full $25,000 credit on the house. We were ecstatic!

This method rarely fails. However, I am always shocked and surprised when it does work. It's good not to know how it works. You have to remember not to be overconfident. Be ready for things not to go your way. This is why the worst-case scenario is so useful. You are preparing yourself for the hardest blow.

Now that I have given many personal examples, I want to provide an example of a worst-case scenario that is on a global scale. Actually, this is more of a national level.

Please note, this is only my opinion. Please have respect before banging your fists on your desk and screaming at the top of your lungs. You just might be upset about what I am about to say.

So, here goes:

2016 election

I believe that the result of the 2016 presidential election between Donald Trump and Hillary Clinton had a lot to do with the worst-case scenario formula.

Let's look at the mindset of the voters of this election. Let's start with the mindset of the voters for Donald Trump.

The voters believed that Donald Trump had a slight chance of winning, but unlikely. Their worst-case scenario was that they were going to live in a Hillary Clinton world. They thought about all the bad things they could think of when imagining a Hillary Clinton world. They thought deeply. All the worst fears were conjured upon their minds. They didn't like this Hillary Clinton world, and they saw this was the worst-case scenario for the 2016 election.

However, were they okay with this worst-case scenario? Remember, being okay with the outcome is the secret ingredient to this worst-case scenario formula. You must be okay with the worst-case scenario that you imagined. I believe the Trump voters were okay with the worst-case scenario.

Many of those voters could check off the box that said, "female president." They could have comfort in knowing that a woman president was in office. They didn't like the current woman running, but they were okay with Hillary because she was a woman. Years of finger-pointing and blame may finally come to an end.

Hillary voters

What was the mindset of the Hillary Clinton voters? They thought Donald Trump was a joke, and he was an annoying flea. He would never be president in a million years, and his supporters are entirely out of their minds. They will come to their senses at voting time.

Every media outlet promised that Hillary Clinton was a shoo-in. It was a slam dunk—nothing to worry about. Hillary's got this in the bag. The election is just a formality. Break out the hats and the champagne. What a wonderful world we live in. God bless us all—and Tiny Tim, too!

Now, I don't have to tell you what happened. Well, for those living under a rock: Donald Trump was victorious.

Hillary Clinton voters failed to imagine a worst-case scenario. They were so confident that Hillary would win that a worst-case scenario wasn't in their wildest dreams.

The candidates

It was not just the voters who had a worst-case scenario imagined. The candidates did too. It was more of not being attached to the outcome or not giving a shit about what happens. Let's look at the candidates.

Donald had an exceptionally good private life before running for office. Although he had flirted with the idea of running for president in the past, he never really took politics all that seriously.

In his mind, being president wasn't all that important. He had a good life outside of politics. Being president didn't define him. It wasn't his identity. He was already a real estate mogul, TV celebrity, and the owner of the Miss Universe pageant. He wasn't that invested in politics.

And it showed. In his mind, if he were going to be president, he would do it his way. He had an "I don't give a shit attitude." He didn't care who he pissed off. He wasn't going to play nice-nice. He was very candid about his policies and didn't hold much back.

In his mind, he was happy that he made it as far as he did. I don't think he expected to make it as far as he did. He always knew he could go back to his former life, so losing wasn't a bad thing. He just wanted to give a shot and have more publicity for himself. He wanted to be on the biggest stage in the world.

But if he lost, he couldn't have given a bigger shit. This is what allowed him to win the election. He didn't give a shit. He was using the Law of Attraction at its best.

Hillary

Now, let's look at Hillary Clinton. Clinton had wrapped up her whole identity in being the first female president. She wanted the position at all costs. She wanted it too badly. She was too tied to the outcome.

If she failed to be president, she would be miserable. She would have to hang out with Bill. She had exhausted all the other opportunities in Washington. She was already secretary of state and a senator of New York. She couldn't take a step backward.

If her opponent won, she wouldn't get a job in the White House anyway.

As we witnessed, she was miserable after the outcome. She wrote a whole book about how she was pissed that she lost the election.

I could write a whole book on how the Law of Attraction played a role in the 2016 election, but I will leave it like that. I think you get the main idea. Don't be too attached to the outcome. The best way to do that is to think of the worst-case scenario and be okay with it.

Conclusion

I believe that worst-case scenario visualization has its place, and positive visualization is overrated.

Remember, I'm not saying that you should think of everything in a worst-case scenario. But only things where you are too attached to a positive outcome. There are two steps. Think of the worst-case scenario and be okay with the result. It's not easy to do, but you will find something.

I'm also not saying you should walk around with a negative attitude.

Also, please note, thinking or visualizing the worst-case is not the same thing as worrying about a bad outcome. They are completely different. I'm sure you know that, but I just wanted to clarify that.

Key takeaways:

- Positive thinking doesn't always work
- Sometimes, you must think about the worst-case scenario
- Thinking about the worst-case scenario is letting your fears go
- The worst-case scenario is a mental rehearsal, so you are prepared for a letdown—basically, you are detaching yourself from the outcome.

-8-

The One Ingredient Hidden Inside You for Ultimate Success

Having the wrong focus just might keep you from getting what you want. Most people who try to manifest their desires often have the wrong focus. They focus on having a massive amount of wealth without any thought of doing anything with it.

The focus should be on your contribution to the world. Some of the wealthiest people got to be wealthy by not focusing on being wealthy but by helping people.

Steve Jobs wanted to make a computer more accessible to the masses. Although his first Macintosh seemed outside of the reach of most people's budget, he fought hard within the Apple management to make the Macintosh as affordable as possible. He believed everyone should have a beautiful and easy-to-use personal computer.

Mark Zuckerberg wanted to connect people all over the world. When the Winklevoss twins wished to have a social network exclusive to Ivy League students, Zuckerberg thought everyone around the world should be connected.

Henry Ford wanted to make cars more affordable to everyone. He paid his workers much more than other car manufacturers.

He even raised their wages in the middle of The Great Depression when everyone else was laying off people and lowering their wages.

Sam Walton built his fortune by making as many products accessible to as many people as possible at prices they could afford. The combined inheritance that his children received is valued at over 150 billion dollars today. That is quite a family fortune that Sam Walton built up with Walmart. He was known to drive around in his red pickup truck. Sam's Ford F-150 Custom was purchased new by Walton in 1979, and he drove it until he died in 1992. Walton is someone who understood the value and wasn't focused on just getting rich.

Warren Buffett still lives in the same modest home he purchased back in 1958 for $32,500—despite being the third richest man in America with over 81 billion dollars. His wealth was not his goal. He loved what he was doing. Why hasn't Buffett moved into a palatial mansion with 20 to 30 rooms? His answer about his current home, "I'm happy there. I'd move if I thought I'd be happier someplace else." There is someone who has the right focus.

Elon Musk has a strong desire to make the world a better place. He believed we should have cars that use clean energy. He was up against some excessively big titans in the automotive industry. He was on a mission. For Space X, he wants to colonize Mars to help all of humanity.

As a young man, John D. Rockefeller said that his two highest ambitions were to make $100,000 and live to be 100. He died two months shy of his 98th birthday, but boy did he make good on the first goal. His fortune at its peak was $318 billion in today's inflation-adjusted dollars. Even though it has been noted that one of his life's ambitions was to make $100,000, he was still a prominent philanthropist. Even while he was only making a modest amount of money, he always gave to charity.

The one thing that is true about all these people is that every one of them never believed they would have made the wealth they had achieved. Every one of them at one time or another said that the fortune they made was way beyond anything they had ever dreamed about or set goals to.

They weren't hyper-focused on the money; they were focused on serving mankind.

After making a massive fortune, Andrew Carnegie still cherished the first modest raise he got as a kid. It was more money than he ever dreamed possible. He was just focused on doing a good job and helping people. Carnegie went on to give away most of his fortune by establishing libraries. He put money toward over 2,500 libraries. He believed in helping all mankind, which was his underlying goal.

Not only did all of these men achieve more than they ever thought possible, but they all gained their wealth much faster than they had ever thought possible.

Sadly, we live in a rush-rush society, and we hear too many marketing messages telling us that we can make fortunes overnight. I fell into this trap for many years. I was so busy trying to make my fortune overnight. It wasn't until I slowed down that I began to see things flow my way quickly.

Patience

The unfortunate thing about seeing all these famous people and their fortunes is that we think wealth should be created overnight. Sadly, a lot of Law of Attraction teachers continue this myth. That will get you nowhere.

If there was anything that I learned in life was to respect time and have patience. When I was a child, a lot of things came easily to me--friends, sports, creative pursuits. As an adult, I expected it to be all the same. However, as an adult, I'm in a much bigger arena with more formidable players, and they all want a piece of the pie.

The more I pursued things with no respect to time, the more times I failed to get respect. I didn't have any patience for the things I was seeking. I expected everything to be done overnight, whether it was learning marketing, advertising, losing weight, improving my diet, improving my mind, gaining wealth,

I had no respect for time. The beauty of having patience and respecting time is that things will happen faster. You just need to have reasonable expectations.

Long-range plans

Most successful people have long-range and realistic goals. And most of these people will also tell you that they reached their goals sooner than they had anticipated.

Unfortunately, there are too many get-rich-quick schemes out there. People are telling you that you can make six figures in six months or have a coaching business pulling in $25,000/month in just three to four months. I'm sure some people can do this, but this shouldn't be an objective. For most people, it's just not realistic.

Remember, your mind is 95% subconscious and 5% conscious. The conscious mind is also known as the ego-mind. You may get pumped up about a business opportunity where you can make $25,000/month or ramp up to six figures in six months. Still, your subconscious mind is saying, "Hey, Bob, do you remember the last time you tried [fill in your answer here]? Well, this is looking a lot like that. I think we should hold back until something else comes along."

Unfortunately, your ego-mind is the mind that gets all the attention. You don't hear your subconscious mind. It's running in the background. You only hear the ego-mind that is all jazzed up about this new opportunity. You do not hear all the rational arguments of why this is a bad idea. You may have some doubts and hesitations, but your ego-mind has been primed to want riches overnight.

This is where manifesting only for money will not work. For instance, if you don't feel worthy of making $25,000 a month coaching people, you will never make that kind of money. No matter what kind of skills you acquire, your subconscious will resist if you don't feel worthy. You must feel it and believe it to make it happen. This is why some people stay stuck. They don't have any realistic long-range plans.

Media

Not only do these get-rich-quick schemes get you to think that fortunes can be made overnight, but the mass media contributes to a lot of how we think about how wealth is created.

Wealth often has a trajectory that looks like a hockey stick curve. It's slow going at first, but then there comes a time where everything takes off fast. However, everyone seems to forget about the slow-going part.

Unfortunately, you don't see this in these success stories. You just see the headlines and how wealth was created practically overnight. You don't see the details of the story. Every success story has details—details that are often overlooked.

I'm not trying to discourage you. I'm just trying to steer your yacht in the right direction. If you focus on opportunity, helping people, and making long-range goals, you will get there faster than you ever thought possible. You will also make more money than you ever thought possible.

For humanity

Zig Ziglar once said, "You can have everything in life you want if you will just help other people get what they want." I found this to be remarkably accurate. Sadly, we are all only looking out for ourselves.

During one of my guided meditations, I was asked what I wanted to manifest. For months and months, I tried to manifest abundance and wealth. Not much happened. When I shifted my focus on manifesting the real me and helping people, a lot of things started to fit into place. I had more job opportunities. Old colleagues called me out of the blue. My relationships with my wife, her family, and my family got better.

Sometimes, you just have to want to be you. Just manifest you. The real you. Focus on contributing to the world. You have to know how you add to the world. You may have no marketable skills. But if you focus on providing to the world, you will find that you will get things much easier and faster than you ever dreamed possible.

This also holds true for finding love. If you only focus on what the other person should be, it will take longer to find what you are looking for. However, if you focus on how you will contribute to the relationship, you will get what you want a lot sooner. Have the mindset of being there for others.

Lack of focus vision boards

Vision boards often have too much stuff. Many Law of Attraction gurus advocate putting a bunch of things on your vision boards.

Focus on your success. Other than winning the lottery, getting an inheritance, marrying into it, or a gift from a benefactor, you will most likely work for your money. When you focus only on the money, you will often question how you will get the money. Many Law of Attraction advocates say, "Don't worry about it. Let the Universe figure it out." That is true to a point. You shouldn't worry about how it all works. However, it still won't stop you from questioning it as you try to manifest your dreams.

When I say focus on your success, you don't have to come up with any particular thing. You may not have any real marketable skills. However, if you focus just on your success, you will start to believe you can have money. You know deep inside that no one gets rich without having success.

Success

Martha Stewart created a billion-dollar fortune by being a homemaker. Wealth can be made through the most mundane means. Colonel Sanders turned his homemade fried chicken recipe into a multimillion-dollar enterprise.

You may not be capable of working. However, you can make wise investments. This is being successful.

If you focus on success rather than money, you will tap into your inner wisdom. Over time, you will see that your inner wisdom or intuition is your greatest asset. You may not realize it now—if you haven't tapped into it—but when you tap into your inner wisdom, you will see how powerful it is and the places it will take you.

When you hear people manifesting great things in their lives, they didn't just plop into their lives without effort. Through the practice of manifesting, they were given opportunities to have great things come into their lives where they didn't have to put in a lot of effort.

But very few things came without some effort. The home I bought was a bargain compared to other homes. I manifested an ideal home for myself and my wife. We got exactly what we wanted at a price that we would have never dreamed possible. Nobody else believes it either! However, we still had to pay money for it. We didn't get it for free. It wasn't given to us.

When Oprah Winfrey interviewed Jim Carrey, he said, "You can't just visualize it and then go eat a sandwich."

Visualization for success allows opportunities to come to you. It doesn't mean you don't do anything. Just like Jim Carrey said, you can't visualize and go eat a sandwich. You must actually do something—unless you're Sam Walton's children. However, if you have nothing and don't expect to get an inheritance, the focus should be on finding opportunities.

Michael Nesmith's mother was a secretary when she invented Liquid Paper for correcting writing and typing mistakes. (By the way, Michael Nesmith was a guitarist for the Monkee's, a sixties TV band. It's a long story). She sold Liquid Paper to the Gillette company for $47.5 million in 1979.

I can't get into the mind of Michael Nesmith's mother, but fortunes can be made by the most unlikely of people and the most unlikely of places. I don't think anyone would have thought in a million years that a creepy kid from Harvard would create a business worth over $500 billion from his dorm room.

Opportunity

Focus on opportunity, not money.

Here's one of my favorite quotes from Carrey:

"I think everybody should get rich and famous and do everything they ever dreamed of so they can see that it's not the answer." – Jim Carrey

If you focus only on money, and you get it, you might feel empty inside. Some of the wealthiest people are often the unhappiest. If you focus on money and don't get it, you will feel frustrated and unhappy.

Focus on the opportunity and what the journey will give. Remember, the Universe wants you to be happy. The Universe won't plop a fortune on your lap if it knows you will become a crack-addicted whore. When you focus on opportunity, you will see things fall into place very quickly.

So, what's the solution? Many Law of Attraction teachers tell you to NOT set a date on whatever you're manifesting. This is sound advice. However, if you don't set any kind of date, you will always be asking the Universe, "Where's my stuff?" Every day, you will be wondering where's your stuff.

You will only get your stuff when you least expect it. In other words, you will only get it when you stop asking for it.

What I found to be useful (and based on what very successful and wealthy people do) is to have a very long-range plan. I set a time and date far in the future of what I want. I still work on manifesting it in the usual way, but I give myself realistic timelines. Like all those successful people mentioned earlier, I find that I get what I asked for a lot sooner than I had expected—and originally asked for.

Setting a date far into the future allows you to stop focusing on the money or the results. It will enable you to focus on the process or what you need to do to get there. You will no longer wonder when it's going to come. You will no longer think it's an unrealistic process.

For instance, let me give you two illustrations.

Say you want to increase your salary to $100,000, but you are only making $50,000. There are some get-rich-quick gurus that will tell you that you can do this in six months. This is basically doubling your income in six months. In the back of your head, in your subconscious, you have never heard of anyone doing this ever. You will naturally have resistance.

Now, if someone more realistically told you that you could increase your income to $100,000 in five years, that would be easier for your subconscious to swallow. If you looked back and realized you never doubled your salary in 5 years, you would welcome the opportunity.

If you are okay with that arrangement and your subconscious is okay with that and believes it to be realistic, then you are closer to manifesting your dreams. You can set your mind on doing that without any negative self-talk. You will, no doubt, reach your goal of making $100,000 faster than five years. You would probably achieve that goal in just one year because you took off all the pressure of trying to do the near-impossible. You focused on your inner wisdom instead.

Here's another illustration

Finding love. Too many people put pressure on themselves to find someone right away. I know I did. I gave you several examples throughout the book. I know too many women (my friends mostly) who are either pressured by family or put pressure on themselves to get married right away. These women have still never been married at the age of 52 and older.

Trying to find love overnight never works. It's too much pressure. Your vibration will be out of alignment. Focus on other things. I know many people in happy marriages that met their spouses when they weren't even thinking about finding love. It was a church outing, a social gathering, a charity event, etc. This is why bars and dating sites don't really work very well. There is too much pressure to make something happen right away.

You are better off joining a club and community activities. Volunteer in your community. I met a lot of hotties when I used to volunteer for Habitat for Humanity home building projects. I also met a lot of close friends.

Have an outward focus. Think about what other people want and how you can serve them. As Zig Ziglar said, you can have anything you want if you help other people get what they want.

Conclusion

When you relax and stop trying to make everything happen overnight, you raise your vibration to the level that will allow you to attract the things you want in your life. However, if you are always looking and waiting and living your life anxiously wondering when something is going to happen, you will be waiting for a long time. If you create a realistic long-range plan to get what you want, you will find that you will get it faster and easier than you ever imagined. That's how the Law of Attraction works.

Key Takeaways:

- Focus on opportunities versus just money
- Think about serving humanity rather than money
- The wealthiest people in America got their wealth by serving people

Action Plan:

If you want to make a $100,000 salary, think long-range. It is much more believable to the subconscious mind. Make a five-year plan to earn $100,000. This will take the pressure of you trying to manifest something quickly.

Here is a helpful script:

First, the request: "I want to make $100,000 / year by October 15, 2025 [or whatever is five years from now]. I am open to new opportunities that will get me closer to my goal. [This is your positive affirmation]. From there, I will make more money year after year."

This long-range view will take the pressure off, and you will have an easier time believing that it could happen. How do you think you will feel if you have an easier time believing it will happen? You will feel pretty good, right? Every day, you will believe more and more that you will increase your salary to $100,000 in five years. If you keep this up, before you know it, you will have increased your salary to $100,000.

-9-

The Short-Cut to Raising Your Vibration and Allowing All Your Desires to Flow to You Quickly

Many people struggle to manifest the things they want into their lives. Nothing comes to them, and they don't know why. They do all the exercises and follow all the advice. They meditate, they journal, they write out what they want and then burn it, they say affirmations, they create visions boards, etc. They do all tricks and gimmicks they were instructed to do and still nothing.

The problem isn't really with the exercise or the formula. The problem is with the person doing them. I would think Harry Potter's magic wand would be utterly useless in anyone else's hands. (Actually, I'm not 100% sure about that since I haven't read the books, and I slept through most of the movies. However, the point is that everything you read about manifesting are just tools to use. They aren't magic wands.)

Most people want tools. They want practical exercises. The biggest sellers of any book in the self-help space are books that offer practical exercises. People don't want to hear about a lot of theory, and they certainly don't want to hear about how that theory relates to making positives changes. They just want to be given exercises to do. This is a shame because it's this theory that is the most practical, not the exercises.

The garbage

To manifest exactly what you want, you need to clear your mind. I'm sure you've heard that before. However, you probably want a practical exercise on how to do just that. You probably want the latest meditation that will give you what you want faster than ever. You probably want a yoga practice that will clear both your mind and body. You probably want the perfect script to manifest a million dollars. Am I right?

The problem is that you are just piling all that good stuff on top of garbage. By garbage, I mean what's going on inside your head. Believe it or not, there is a lot of waste in there.

Yes, you've cleared your blocks during some meditation. But have you? And if you have, did you really get rid of the garbage?

Trying to manifest anything with the tools provided with all the garbage in your head is like building a new home with the most advanced hardware while using rotten lumber. The best hardware in the world will not build a house with rotten lumber.

Where does this garbage come from? It comes mostly from what we consume daily. I am not talking about food or water. I am talking about toxic media. However, it goes beyond that, but I will go into that later. Let's first start with what you see on your television.

The news

The news is highly toxic to your mental well-being and offers almost no value to you whatsoever. Watching CNN, MSNBC, and Fox News is like having a diet of Oreos and fried cheese and expecting to lose weight and never have a heart attack or get diabetes.

The news capitalizes on your most primal instinct, and your most primal instinct is to survive as long as possible. That is what the human mind is designed to do. You are designed to survive at all costs. There are amazing stories of people's will to survive in awful circumstances. Nazi death camps are just one example.

The news knows your strong desire to survive at all costs. So, what do they do? They manipulate you into believing that your survival depends on your being informed by their news' broadcasts.

This is how we survive. We survive by knowing what is going to kill us. Some of this is so primal that we are born with it—no need to learn it from our parents or society. Babies instinctively know that they could drown in water. Unfortunately, that's about it. Human babies have extremely poor innate survival instincts.

Most of our fears and what we need to know for survival are learned. From the day we are born until the day we die, we are continually learning about what's gonna kill us. When we are young, we learn this mostly from our parents and guardians.

"Little Johnny, get your finger out that socket!"

"Eric Thomas Jenkins, this is the last time I am going to tell you to get off that ledge!"

Every single day we are vigilant about what's gonna kill us and what won't. *"This slice of ham looks green. It must be bad. Throw it out! That slice of ham is pink and looks a lot like my ass cheek pressed up against the window. It must be okay. Give me two servings, please!"* Decisions like these are made every second of our lives.

Information is what helps us survive. We need information. This is especially true in the Information Age. No longer are we walking around with clubs and spears to protect us. We rely on our instincts and knowledge more than ever. We know from trial and error that a car will kill us if we walk in front of one.

So, where do we get this information? If it doesn't come from our close circle of family and friends, we usually get this information from the media. More people are tuned into the media than ever before. And they rely on this information from the media to help them survive.

This is why stories about plane crashes get high ratings. People want to know the facts so that they can protect themselves. The scenario goes something like this:

What kind of plane was it? Commercial or private?

Private? I don't fly in those. I don't need to hear this. I'll turn off the TV.

Commercial airliner? I fly all the time on commercial. I better listen up.

What kind of airplane? 787? Note to self: Don't fly a 787.

What airline was it? American Airlines? Note to self: Don't fly American Airlines. Fly United instead. Oh, they beat people up and drag them off the plane? Try Delta.

How did it happen? It flew over a volcano. I only fly within the continental United States, so no worry about volcanoes.

Pilot error or mechanical error?

Pilot error? I better make sure my pilot isn't at the bar having cocktails before I board the plane.

Mechanical error? The next time I fly, I better look out my airplane window to see if there are more maintenance trucks than usual.

And this little checklist goes on and on in your head as you watch a broadcast about a plane crash. You want to know the facts so that you can plan your next move. This will help you survive the next air disaster.

Sadly, this really doesn't help much. You could avoid all air travel and still die. Yes, avoiding all air travel would certainly keep you from dying in a plane crash—unless one crashes into your house.

However, that isn't very practical for most people. If you did avoid all air travel, you are not immune to dying in a car, a truck, a bus, a motorcycle, a plane, a ship, a boat, a yacht, a bicycle, a scooter, a crosswalk, a skateboard, or any other mode of transportation. As you can see, tuning into TV for every air disaster (to gather information) doesn't solve your ultimate problem: not dying.

Tuning into the TV to watch every air disaster only really accomplishes one thing: messing up your mind. While you may not get anxiety, you will have a level of vibration that is not conducive to manifesting your dream life.

Airplane disasters are just one small example of many. On television, you will witness school shootings, workplace shootings, violent protests, nasty politics, peculiar household accidents, war, famine, Walmart fights, etc. It would be tough to raise your vibration with all this darkness in your head. Wouldn't you agree?

Unfortunately, we are drawn to these disasters like moths to a flame or flies to dog shit.

The question is: *Why?*

As discussed, it is a survival mode.

And the mainstream media knows this. There was a quote from an old movie about network news. It went like this: "If it bleeds, it leads." In other words, if it has blood and gore, it is the first thing to air on the upcoming news broadcast. This will keep people from turning the channel.

But are we really into blood and gore just for the hell of it? No, it's our survival mechanism kicking in.

NOT being informed

Let's be clear; the news is not there to inform you. That kind of journalism died ages ago (if it ever existed). Today, we have money-hungry media that will stop at nothing to keep you glued to the TV.

They're NOT informing you of anything that will help you survive. They only cause you more stress. Stress has been linked to nearly every chronic disease.

There are thousands of articles regarding the link between chronic health conditions and stress. These health conditions include diabetes, heart disease, kidney disease, cancer, and lupus, to name a few. Hundreds of studies categorically say stress is a significant factor in these diseases and early death.

The one thing about these chronic diseases is that they are all preventable. With medical advancements in our modern society, we can cure and prevent many deadly contagious diseases and acute illnesses. We have a fantastic ability to repair anything broken. Each of us could live over one hundred years. However, it's the stress that's killing us early.

Stop watching the news. They are wrong nearly all the time, and they lie to keep you tuned in.

I lost my magic abilities

When I was young—the years before graduating from college and entering the real world—I had a lot of magic abilities. I just didn't know it then. But when I look back on those years, I had made many things happen in my life that many would classify as coincidence, or serendipity, or simply good fortune. At the time, I believed that was exactly what it was. Looking back, I realize that by being me and having a higher vibration, I was making those things happen to and for me.

Many of my friends and classmates would often comment that everything just worked out for me. Looking back, I guess they did.

When I was living in Texas, I called in sick for a job I hated. From the first few hours that I was home 'sick,' I was thankful I wasn't at work. However, at around 10:00 o'clock in the morning, I was getting bored. I wanted to go to work, but I had already told them I was sick.

I was really upset with myself for playing the sick card. While I sat at home, I had wished that something would happen that would justify me staying at home and pretending to be sick. About an hour later, there was a huge hailstorm outside.

The hail was the size of golf balls. I looked out the window and saw this golf ball-sized hail pounding the street, the parking lot, and the grass. I saw the hail pounding on the tin roof of the covered parking area provided by the apartment complex I had been living in.

I was thankful that my car was under the covered parking. I realized that if I had gone to work, I would have parked my car outside in the open. I would have been pelted by hail.

The next day I went to work. Every person that I worked with had hail damage to their car. They either had broken windshields, and/or their vehicle looked like a golf ball with dimples all over. I felt good and bad at the same time. I felt good that my car was not damaged, but I felt terrible that my coworkers all had destroyed vehicles.

Most people would dismiss this as good fortune or a coincidence. I choose to believe otherwise.

Sadly, as I joined the working world, things got serious. My life got a little more serious with added responsibilities. Even with the added responsibilities, it seemed as if I had more idle time. When I was in college, I was living in dormitories and in apartments with my friends. There was no time to watch TV except for Saturday and Sunday football games.

When I got out of college, I was living alone. I spent much of my time watching late-night TV and cable news. This was the beginning of lowering my vibration. Things started to become harder, and I struggled more. I no longer had the magic touch.

I felt sadder. I couldn't find meaningful connections and relationships. I watched more and more TV and sank in deeper and deeper into depression.

Looking back on it now, I can see how the news corrupted my mind. It made me depressed and worried about my future. I was worried about my future. Most of it needlessly. I had a good job and not many responsibilities. It should have been a very magical time for me, but it wasn't. I wasn't married, and no kids or pets, so no duties there. However, I was always worried.

I came from a good supportive family, although at times, there was conflict. However, I worried about a lot of stuff often.

I now realize how much the news played a role in that. It wasn't just the network news. I also watched shows like *Dateline* and *20/20*. I would watch these shows every chance I got. Sady, these shows always made it sound like whatever they were talking about could happen to *you*.

They would always something like, "What would you do if this happened to *you*?" My conscious mind would often ignore that. However, when those words were pumped into my brain week after week, my subconscious mind started to absorb them and believe them. What if I did get stuck in a tree during a torrential rainstorm? What would I do? What if I were pregnant and I was about to give birth to two-headed twins? What would I do? What *would* I do if my arm got stuck between two boulders?

On and on it went with these worst-case scenarios and what I would do if it happened to me. Every show scratched a little more out of my brain. Just a little. Very little. Just like a casino. It takes just a little off the top, but then it multiplies it into big fortunes. That's what this news was doing to me. It was just taking a little each day over time to have an overall damaging effect on me.

News biased to please sponsors

I watched one news broadcast where they brought in a nutritionist to talk about having a nutritional diet. When the nutritionist said that we should all stay away from Coca-Cola, the news broadcaster got here back up and insisted that avoiding Coke was too drastic. The scene went something like this:

News reporter: "What are some things people should avoid in their diets?"

Nutritionist: "Sodas are a big no-no. They can—"

News reporter: "You mean we should drink more diet sodas."

Nutritionist: "No, all sodas. Regular sodas are loaded with sugar, and diet sodas are no better. They are filled with—"

News reporter: "So, you mean we should cut down on how much we drink."

Nutritionist: "We should eliminate them altogether."

News reporter: "You mean, a little is okay."

Nutritionist: "No. Sodas are loaded with sugar and contributes to obesity and—"

News reporter: "But not everyone is at risk for obesity."

Nutritionist [stumped]: "I guess, but too much sugar contributes to diabetes."

News reporter: "So, we should have only one or two sodas a day."

Nutritionist: "No, I'm saying that we should not drink sodas at all for a healthy diet and lifestyle."

News reporter: "Okay, we'll see about that." [Looking into the camera and reading the next story] "Can a walrus really jump through a hoop like a dolphin? Find out when we come back."

You will never get the truth from the news, so don't bother trying. They need to please their sponsors. That's the game. And they will instill their derision every chance they get. This is what gets people to tune in, and their sponsors love it.

This is an outright form of lying. The news is lying to you. Would you hang out with friends if they were constantly lying to you? Think about that the next time you tune in to the news.

The conflict games

The conflict game between Fox News and CNN, MSNBC, is won by all media. You end up being the loser in this fake conflict. Let's not forget that these news outlets are merely different sides of the same coin. They will find and invent conflict because conflict keeps people tuned in. It's a never-ending contest. Imagine a football game or a tennis match that never ends—the tide of winning ebbs and flows, but there is never any resolution. You think that there might be a resolution coming soon, but it doesn't come. They don't want resolution because they want to keep you tuned in.

There are no winners or losers between Fox News (CNN) and their counterparts. The only loser is you. You are a victim of their conflict game, and you are the one who is hurt by their conflict. They are the ones who make butt loads of money by keeping you tuned in day after day. They are the ones who grow their empires.

Meanwhile, you get stuck in depression, anxiety, and perpetual "fight or flight" mode. You are the one who is left to pick up the pieces of their conflict.

Every time you are in fight or flight mode, you are about as far away from manifesting your dream as you possibly can get. This highly agitated state will keep everything you ever wanted from you.

Emotional addiction

So, why do we watch so much?

We keep tuning in because we are addicted to the emotions that the news churns up. It feels good when someone confirms something that we believe in. Believe it or not, it even feels good to be angry at something. Whether it overtly makes us happy or miserable, we are still addicted to the emotions that we conjure up.

Many people classify themselves as "news junkies."

By constantly watching the news, you are lowering your vibrational energy. Being angry and upset all the time will keep your subconscious in turmoil.

The government

Cable news such as Fox News and CNN report a lot about politics. The sad part is that too many people make the government such an essential part of their lives. This is obviously brought upon by these news networks.

Our founding fathers set out to make the federal government as less intrusive as possible. They didn't want it to be significant or important. They looked at the federal government almost as a necessary evil. Sadly, the news has put an emphasis on government.

Don't put so much importance on the government. The Universe is bigger—much bigger. Look at some photos from Hubble Telescope, and you will see how big the Universe is. Wouldn't you rather be aligned with the Universe than with your government? Stop minding the government and start minding Universe.

The Universe is much bigger than the government. Start minding the Universe.

Conclusion:

It's hard to manifest the good things in your life when your mind is full of toxins. Most of this garbage comes from the news. Even if you don't watch it directly, the information may be in the form of talking with your friends or social media.

The news makes money by capitalizing on your most basic primal instinct. That instinct is to gather information to ward off some unfortunate future event. Unless you act on this information, you will only end up raising your stress level. You will also be out of vibrational alignment with the Universe.

The good news is that you can fix your toxic mind and get more vibrationally aligned with the Universe. Just turn off the news. If you do this, you will be miles ahead. Doing this one thing will raise your vibration—allowing you to manifest the good things in life. It's nearly impossible to manifest the good things in life if your head is filled with the bad things in life.

Key Takeaways:

- Clear your toxin brain for higher vibrational alignment
- The news is not your friend. It preys upon your primal fears
- Turn off the news to raise your vibration
- The Universe is MUCH bigger than the government

Action Plan:

Stop watching the news. If an event is really that important to you, you will find out somehow. As long as you are in tune with the Universe, you will know what to know without watching the news.

Limit your news watching to one hour a week. The news is so repetitive that you will see the most important things you need to see in the first fifteen minutes.

Think about how important the news is to you. Has your life been that much better by knowing about every political strife, plane crash, suicide bombing, and school shooting? And more importantly, how have you changed your life because of your knowledge of all these events? Have you made it necessary to vote in every election, even for the officials in your town? Have you avoided flying on airplanes? Have you made it a point not to travel to countries on your bucket list because there is a rise in suicide bombings? Have you decided to pull your children out of school and have them homeschooled?

Unless you act on the news that you hear, it only stresses you out. You haven't really gained anything from the information you got from the news unless you have taken corrective action. Just listening to the news and not doing anything will raise your anxiety. You may not feel it, but it will lower your vibrations and your connection to the Universe.

With all the free time you have gained, you can now focus on what you do want instead of watching on screen all the things you don't want. You can concentrate on meditations, writing in your journals, raising your vibrations, and anything else that will bring you what you want.

-10-

9 Practical Exercises to Quickly Manifest Your Most Elusive Desires

Here are a few practical exercises that I have used with great success.

1. Keep track of wins

Keeping track of your wins is a great way to appreciate where you are now and shows how far you have come. These can be wins in your life; for instance, you just got an interview or landed a date. Keeping track of what you are achieving in life is vital to having success in your life. Many successful people have a daily or weekly accounting of their accomplishments. They keep track of their wins.

The problem with most people—especially those attracted to the Law of Attraction principles—is that they want everything overnight and easy. They see the success that other people have as an overnight success; therefore, they have those expectations. They don't see the micro successes that successful people have had leading up to the big success.

Keeping a journal of your daily and weekly wins will show you that small incremental successes are how people become successful in life.

You could call this journal your *Wins Journal*. It's up to you. It doesn't matter what you name it. Once you create this journal and keep track of your wins, you will see that you are making forward progress in your life. You will know that you are swimming with the current instead of against it.

Recording your wins and reviewing them later helps you appreciate the things you have accomplished. This also makes it easier to ask for more wins and stuff. Overall, you will feel more confident and more at ease. One of the cornerstones of successful manifestations is to be relaxed and at ease.

You've already asked the Universe for what you want. You just need to recognize and appreciate what you have already received. When you do that—by keeping this journal—you will continue to receive more. Keeping track of your daily and weekly wins is a great way to do just that.

2. Journal of Magic

I have a journal where I keep track of every little magic thing that has happened to me. When you start to see and recognize the magic around you, you will begin to have confidence in your magical abilities. Your eyes will open to how the Universe works.

One of your journal entries could be, "I asked the Universe for $5, and today, I found a five-dollar bill sitting in a grocery cart."

This is one of the best things I have done on my journey to be more in tune with the Universe and manifest things in my life. Often when we get caught up in our daily lives, we don't see things as being remarkable. We just see them as coincidences, odd occurrences, or just getting lucky.

However, if you see them as *you* make things happen, you will know that you are indeed communicating with the Universe.

This is what I wrote down in my journal just the other day:

"The Universe showed me a sign today. I had three containers of blueberries in the refrigerator. I had lamented that I had too many containers of blueberries. I wouldn't be able to eat that many before they go bad. I couldn't understand how I ended up with three containers instead of just two.

Right after that thought entered my mind, I dropped one of the containers onto the floor spilling blueberries everywhere. I now have two containers of blueberries—which is what I wanted from the beginning. The Universe speaks in mysterious ways."

As you can see, it's very mundane, and it may not even be divine or mystical, but I choose to see it that way. Seeing things in this magical way helps you realize that there is a Universe that is aware and listening to you. It is real.

Here's another entry I made:

> "Magic Moment [I often title these 'Magic Moment']: The other day, just on a whim, I asked for $5,900 for no particular reason. I didn't care if I got it or not. Today, I got a check for $7,215. It was somewhat expected because my broker told me they sold some of my stock, but I didn't expect to get a check. I just thought it was going to be re-

invested automatically—as it usually is. The real spooky thing is that I got the check one day after asking for $5,900."

I record every event that's hard to explain. As you can see from the entry above, someone could easily explain away these events as coincidences. I choose not to.

In the example above, I was due to get the money (although I wasn't aware of it), and the amounts don't match up. Most people would dismiss that and say that it wasn't a Magic Moment. They would say that the Universe wasn't speaking to me.

However, the more that I recorded these events, the more that these events occurred. And the more that these events occurred, the more I had confidence in my ability to make things happen.

Like I said earlier, creating and writing in this journal is one of the biggest things that allowed me to manifest so much more in my life. When I recognized the magic that was happening around me, the more I believed there was a benevolent Universe listening to me.

Observe, recognize, and appreciate

It's essential to recognize as many magical moments as you possibly can. This will exercise your manifestation muscle. The more you use your manifestation muscle, the more things happen to you.

The downside is when so many things happen to you (that you can't explain logically), it's hard to keep up with your journaling. When bigger things happen (like getting an unexpected check), you start to dismiss the smaller items (like getting the last parking space or dropping a container of blueberries). However, you should try to record every magic moment that comes your way.

Soon, you will see magic moments everywhere. No longer will you see them as mere coincidences, synchronicities, or serendipitous moments.

Here's another entry in my *Journal of Magic*. Some may see this as mundane, but I see it as my magic working all the time.

> "Magic Moment. Just today, I put an extra $2,300 on my list of wants. This evening Tina came to me with a check for $4,400 from our landlady. We had just officially moved out of our rental house a week ago. The whole time while we were renting, we thought we would not get our full damage deposit back. Most landlords come up with some reason not to return the deposit—or any portion of it."
>
> "This morning, I meditated for a few minutes and asked for an extra $2,300. I was 'okay' with a worst-case scenario—such as a bill for $2,300. Then I put it out of my mind."
>
> "This was unexpected—and so soon. Our landlady was notorious for being cheap. We thought we would have to make a strong case for ourselves or even go to small claims court. The check came just a few days after we moved out. There was no note or anything. Just a check in an envelope. Very strange. And quite magical!"

That was my journal entry precisely as written. What I find remarkable was how the numbers work out. The $2,300 is almost exactly half of the check that *we* got from our landlady. The check was for $4,400 for my wife and me. If I had taken my half out of it, it would come to $2,200—which is close to the $2,300 that I had asked for.

Like I said in my journal entry, we did not expect to get our full damage deposit back. Most landlords keep at least half of it. Although we left the house exceptionally clean, some walls had scuff marks and needed to be repainted. My wife and I were both shocked that we got our full damage deposit back. I owe it to the Universe that my request was granted. That's precisely why I put it in my journal.

Every little success with magic should be logged. Soon, you will only enter the big successes—like getting your dream home or tropical island vacation. However, if you have smaller magic moments, you should still try to squeeze them in.

The importance of this journal to have the feeling of, "If I did it once, I could do it again." If you don't see, recognize, and record your successes, you won't know if you can do it again. This is precisely the attitude that multimillionaires have who had made millions of dollars and lost it all. Their position is, "If I can do it once, I can do it again."

3. Gratitude Journal

Many spiritual advisors say you should have a gratitude journal. I am no different. I don't have much to say about this because it has already been said. However, I would like to emphasize that if you miss a day, you should not freak out or think you "messed up."

Many people think if they missed a day of journaling that they messed up their manifestation. Remember, your manifestations are a result of what you believe. That's it. A gratitude journal helps you get in the right mindset and raise your vibration to match your desires.

It's good to have a daily practice. If you practice every day, you are unlikely to miss a day. It will be a daily habit that will be hard to break. Soon, you will feel uncomfortable NOT writing in your journal. That's when you know if you have solidified the habit.

4. Other journals

I have other smaller journals that I write in. While trying to manifest something new, I would create a specific journal for that. For instance, when I was trying to land a new exceptional job, I created a new journal called *Job*. It was kind of a combination of the journals mentioned above plus some affirmations thrown in.

I would write down the wins that I had specifically for my job hunt. By the way, this journal could replace your *Wins Journal*. I also entered "magic moments"—such as getting a call from a classmate that I hadn't heard from in 20 years with a connection to a job I was seeking. It is strange how these things happen.

I wrote down what I wanted in a new job. At the beginning of the journal, I wrote down what I was looking for in a new job. It was a simple two-sentence statement. It went like this:

> "I'm looking for a job that brings me a great amount of satisfaction. The people are nice, and the pay allows me to live comfortably."

Notice, I didn't put in any specifics such as a half-hour commute or $125,000 a year. The Universe knows better than me what a pleasant commute is or what salary is right for me. We will explore this more later.

After my simple request, I wrote down all the blocks I was having. These were the blocks that were keeping me from having an incredible job that I would love and paid me well.

After writing in this journal for just a few weeks, I landed the perfect job at the time. I had since moved on. Below are some excerpts from my *New Job Journal*.

List of blocks

First, I wrote a title for my blocks. In this case, it was *What do I fear about having a full-time job?* Then I wrote out a list of blocks I was having.

What do I fear about having a full-time job?

1. Getting let go (fired)
2. Not being good at my job
3. Getting sucky assignments—assignments I don't feel passionate about
4. Having an asshole boss
5. Having sucky co-workers—people that are out to get me
6. Feeling too old—out of touch
7. Being found out—about my portfolio, testimonials—not being good enough
8. Too much work
9. Agreeing to projects that are too much or I don't like
10. I won't have the energy

11. I will appear stupid
12. Just when things are going well, something terrible will happen
13. Young whipper-snappers
14. The more I make (salary), the more responsibility I will have
15. If I make $120,000, I will have too much responsibility
16. If I make a lot of money, people will think I don't deserve that
17. I look old, fat, ugly, unattractive
18. Intimidated by authority figures
19. Not having KPI's or stats
20. There aren't any jobs
21. I will lose my sense of self
22. I will make other people feel bad
23. I will act like an asshole
24. I won't recognize the opportunity when it presents itself
25. I worry that I am applying for the wrong job
26. Am I hirable/employable?
27. My past employment sucks
28. Nobody wants me
29. I will get nervous during an interview and sweat
30. I won't like the people

It's essential to write down your list of blocks. These are all the things that are keeping you from getting what you want. You may have these blocks swimming around in your head, but you won't properly deal with them unless you write them down and explore them.

You need to recognize what is blocking you from getting what you want. This will allow you to gain confidence in manifesting all that you desire. If you don't dig deep and find the blocks, you will have a harder time manifesting whatever you want.

Review your blocks

Writing down your blocks provides a tremendous release of pressure. After you have written them down, go over them one at a time and think about each one for a few seconds. Since I had a long list, I would only study 5 – 10 of them each day. It was too hard to do all thirty every day. I wanted only to spend at least fifteen seconds each, and I wanted to acknowledge and embrace each block fully.

I would study them and go over them before writing in my journal. After each block, I would say, "That's no big deal. That's okay."

For instance, I would read "Getting fired" as my first block, then I would say to myself, "That's okay. Everyone gets fired. At least I had the [manifested] job. Tina will understand. I just won't mention it on the next job I apply for."

It was vital for me to acknowledge my blocks fully. For this entry, I had been fired or laid off from previous jobs. Some were my fault, and some not. Since I had been married to Tina, I had a few contract jobs that ended early. Often, I was out of work for a while. I felt ashamed for not having a job and bringing in an income. This put a strain on our marriage.

It was important for me not to let this be a block that was keeping me from manifesting the perfect job. My wife must have picked up on this because she told me not to worry if I get a job and then got fired. It wasn't meant to be. Although it was nice to have her support, it was still a big mental block for me.

I needed to acknowledge the possibility of getting fired and being okay with it. I needed to recognize that no job is perfect, and no job lasts forever. I needed to embrace the idea that I could get fired and that it was no big deal—with or without my wife's blessing.

She wasn't the only person I was worried about. I also had hang-ups about what my family and friends would think about me getting fired from a job. Also, any new job that I applied for in the future would want to know what happened at my last job.

I had to be okay with getting fired. This was a major mental block for finding a new job. It's not unlike someone trying to find new love after a painful divorce. They want a new loved one to come to them, but the separation is a mental block that keeps that from happening.

I have a friend in precisely this situation. He had been married for 12 years and then had a bitter divorce. He was so hung up on his ex-wife that he didn't allow someone new to come into his life for fear of going down that road again. Consciously, he was over his wife and his divorce. He wanted to move on, but subconsciously, he was holding back. Although he dated a lot of nice women, he let his mental blocks get the best of him. He is still just flailing around.

This is exactly what happened to me. I had too many jobs that didn't go anywhere, and I started to feel bad about myself. I was afraid of having a full-time job. I had been a freelance writer for a while, so that route seemed safer. I couldn't get fired. I did okay with my freelance career, but I wanted something more secure with health benefits and a steady income. Unfortunately, when it came to finding a full-time job, I had too many mental blocks keeping me from doing just that.

Writing down my blocks made an enormous difference. Not only was it a big help, but it was mandatory. If I didn't sort out my mental blocks, I would have never manifested the exact job that I had gotten shortly after I started my *New Job Journal*.

After reading and studying about 5-10 of my blocks, I would begin to write in my journal for the day. I would write out what kind of job would give me the greatest joy. I also wrote down how I visualized how the whole process would go.

Here is one of my journal entries:

> "I love my job! My boss is great. My co-workers are great. I aced the interview. I answered all their questions to their delight. They loved what I had to say about copywriting. I am so knowledgeable about copywriting that I was able to answer their questions quite easily. My commute is awesome. It is the easiest commute and the most enjoyable commute I've ever had. My job pays me very well. I am so grateful that I make so much money in this new job. It allows me to go on vacation and pay my bills with ease. I love the work that I do. I'm able to help so many people. I can help them with their problems. If money were no object, I would do this job for free. But I gotta live! The hours are great. I get to come and go as I please. No one asks any questions. I don't worry about what they think because I always do a great job. They are incredibly pleased with my work. I get compliments all the time."

I wrote mainly the same thing with different wordings every single morning until I got the job. I had about 21 entries before I got the job. The job turned about to be pretty much everything that I had transcribed.

The commute was easy, considering where I live. The people were super friendly, and no one was out to get me. This was so important because I had so many jobs where my co-workers were out to get me. They were jealous of the work I did and wanted to get me out of there. This job that I manifested was almost too easy.

(Please note: This is the same job that I used the worst-case scenario on. As I said in that chapter, the worst-case scenario is incident-based. In other words, it works when there is a specific event you want to go well, but you have fears of it not going well. This is different than having a journal such as this one where I am raising my vibration. I hope that clears up everything.)

No interview

Also, I had requested that I didn't want to fill out a job application or go chasing after some company or be in a pool of a dozen applicants. I find that the whole process is somewhat degrading.

Again, the Universe was listening. The CEO called me directly and wanted me to come in for an interview. No application bullshit. No phone screening. No nonsense. This is precisely what I spelled out in many of my journal entries.

Raise your confidence

It should be emphasized that this process—and any manifesting technique—is all about raising your confidence (or vibration). The Universe is within you. Therefore, you can't get this wrong. There is no wrong or right way of doing this. You must do things that raise your confidence level and raise your vibration to match what you are seeking.

It's all about belief. Do you believe what you want to be true? If not, then you need to find ways to either raise your confidence or lower your expectations and desires. It will be an uphill battle if you don't have total belief in yourself and what you are doing.

Some spiritual teachers say it's just as easy to manifest $ 5 million as it is to manifest $5. It all depends on where you are coming from and what you believe to be true. If you were a billionaire, then manifesting $5 million would be just as easy as manifesting $5. If you've never seen a few hundred thousand in your life, then it would be tough to manifest $5 million. As discussed previously, there is nothing wrong with starting small to raise your confidence level.

The reason for writing these journal entries is to rewire your brain. You are programming your subconscious. Your subconscious has already been programmed—with a bunch of bad shit when you were young. You've been told there are not enough jobs to go around. You've been told you aren't worthy of having a beautiful life. You have been told that you aren't meant to find the love of your life.

It's time to rewrite those old programs. The best way to do that is by repetition. Just like you can drive a car without thinking about it, you can rewire your brain so you can assume you are successful long before you have seen any real evidence that you are successful.

The journaling allows that to happen. You can rewire your brain to work on automatic pilot. Why are some people successful, and some aren't? It all comes down to the wiring. Some people are wired to feel extraordinarily successful. Some people are wired not to feel successful. But we all breathe the same air, and we all drink the same water, and we all work within the same 24 hours. We all must abide by the same laws of physics.

Don't be fooled by the money. People have made more fortunes with no money than from people who came from money. Not having money is not a factor in becoming wealthy and successful. Not having the right mindset is.

Journaling will change your mindset. That's what it's for. Nothing else. It's not a petition to the Universe. It's about changing your beliefs about yourself. That's it.

5. Meditation

Meditation is another tool I use to help me feel like I have magical powers. Notice that I said "feel like" instead of "have" when referring to magical powers. The feeling comes first.

I don't use the meditations necessary to manifest anything. I use meditation to center myself and to be the best person I can be.

I have written several books on suffering from ectopic heartbeats (heart palpitations). This was a condition I had for a long time, and meditation helped me cure myself.

I say all this because there are a lot of Law of Attraction gurus who have meditations specifically on manifesting what you want. I haven't found that these worked for me. My sole goal was to raise my vibration so I could be a magnet for the good things in life. It felt as if some of those guided meditations were too much "asking."

I prefer not to ask but to just be. This has helped me with a lot of bigger things. Yes, I did think about the things I wanted, like a job and a house. But it really came down to me just being rather than asking.

If you never meditated before, I suggest you start slowly. First, start with just one or two minutes for a week. Then five minutes. Then move up to ten minutes. Soon, you will be able to meditate for a good forty-five minutes to an hour.

6. Everything is going my way

Here's another exercise I would do to elevate my vibration. I would pick a day and promise myself that I would have an elevated emotion of everything going my way. I would try to keep that high emotion all day long. It didn't matter what happened; I always made it seem that it was meant to be that way.

Give it a try!

For one week, you are going to say and believe that everything is going your way. You are going to make a plan that everything is going your way. You are going to think everything is going your way. You are going to write down that everything is going your way.

Then you will record the results.

And when you hit a bump in the road, you will chalk it up to a "steppingstone."

The best way to proceed with this is to create a plan. Don't just jump into this right away. You must plan this out because, during any given week, you will encounter multiple problems and challenges. You need to overcome or ignore these issues; therefore, proper planning is a must.

It's best to write out what you are going to do.

When you first start, just think, feel, and maybe even say a bunch of times, "Everything is going my way today." And if you encounter some problem, just say, "That's no big deal. It's just a stepping stone toward my ultimate goal."

If you plan this for just a week, you will be able to take the pressure off after you have done your assignment. Even though this assignment is one week long, if done correctly, you will find that things really will start going your way in just a few days. However, you should begin the week as if it will take a week or longer. It's better to have measured expectations.

If one week is too long to keep up this higher vibration, then try for one day. Give it your all. As you wake up, just say, "Everything is going my way." You will soon see the magic happening. Be sure to recognize the small things, such as the shower warmed up faster than usual. Someone made breakfast for you. Your favorite pants are clean.

And for everything that goes wrong, just laugh about it. If the shower takes extra long to get warm, just say, "That's normal.

Nothing to worry about there. It doesn't bother me because everything is going my way!" If you get bad news, just say, "It's not as bad as it seems. Things like this happen all the time. Everything is going my way."

7. Exactly as planned

"Exactly as planned" is similar to "everything is going my way." Your life may not be perfect right now, but you are still alive and well enough to read this book. That's a better place than where you could be.

I used to look at my past with a lot of regrets. Now, I look at my life as something that brought me to this point. I was meant to be exactly where I am now.

This new attitude has helped me raise my vibration with the Universe. And it has certainly helped me manifest more things than I ever imagined.

Think of every mishap as going "exactly as planned."

8. Sleepytime gratitude

I have a ritual that helps me take my mind off the events of the day and have a heightened appreciation for what I have and what I've done.

When I write in my gratitude journal, I tend to write about things that are currently happening in my world. This is because I've already covered my past events that I have a great appreciation for.

Instead of writing, "I appreciate it was a sunny day today," or "I appreciate that John gave me a few dollars for coffee today," I will go more in-depth with this exercise. And since you won't have to write anything down, it will be much more pleasant to go much deeper.

This exercise is to appreciate things you have or have had in the past while you are in bed and drifting off to sleep. I found that I am enjoying these things more when I am gently drifting off to sleep.

Instead of thinking about my next vacation—say to Hawaii—I spend the time appreciating my last vacation to Barbados. I started to realize that fantasizing about a holiday that has not been planned is just me continuously asking. And we all know that's not how you get what you want.

Like the example that I gave earlier in the *Aunt & Uncle Bridge*, imagine you gave gifts to your nephews and nieces. What would give you more joy:

1. Your nieces and nephews are always asking you for the next gift shortly after receiving the most recent gift you gave them.
2. Your nieces and nephews are talking endlessly about how much they love and appreciate the most recent gift you gave them.

I think the answer is obvious. You would have more joy with scenario #2. You are more likely to continue giving gifts if you are showered with appreciation regarding the gifts you had given. And you may even make your gifts more extravagant just to get more of a dopamine hit.

This holds true with what you are asking the Universe for. If you don't appreciate what you have, the Universe may not want to keep giving you stuff. If you keep asking, you will just sound like a whiny, spoiled child.

So, instead of thinking about your next beach vacation, appreciate the last beach vacation you took. If what you are asking for is way beyond what you've had in the past, that's okay. Let's say you wanted to go to the Grand Canyon or some other beautiful national park. That may be a big deal to you. The fact that you want to do that means you just asked for it, so you don't need to do any more asking. The Universe knows what you want.

It's time to appreciate what you've done in the past. Now is the time to enjoy the overnight camping trip you took with your child's camping group two summers ago. When you are in bed, lulling yourself to sleep, you can really explore and heighten your emotions. Sometimes writing all this down can become tedious. But when you just think about it in bed, you can really raise your feelings. You can go as far as you can take it.

You can think about the camaraderie you had with the other parents on your child's camping trip. You can think about the joy you see on the faces of the children. Really dive deep. Appreciate the smell of the campfire. Appreciate all the effort that the organizers put into organizing the event. Have a deep appreciation. Be careful not to get all sad nostalgic about it. Love your gifts then and now.

Don't lament

You must be careful about not lamenting or longing for the past. This can lead to a depressed state. In other words, you can get caught up in thinking about how things used to be, and they are not like that now.

It's important to appreciate the event that happened in the past and recognize that things are different now, and acknowledge that things will change in the future. You must be okay with the past being the past. Don't get all sad about the past. Appreciate the gifts you were given in the past.

Using the example above, it would be easy to look at your life right now and think you don't have the money or the means to take a trip to the Grand Canyon. And if you thought about a nice trip you took in the past—say it was paid for by someone—you could easily get caught up in feeling bad that you can't afford a trip like this now.

However, don't do this. You will not be rewarded for such thoughts. Don't get caught up in being nostalgic about the past and not appreciating your life now. You must genuinely appreciate the camping trip you took and really appreciate the joy you had at that time.

This holds true with anything. You may want a new car right now but can't afford one. Instead of wishing for one and feeling bad that you don't have one. Appreciate a vehicle you had in the past. Maybe your parents gave you an old clunker when you were in college. Even though it was an old clunker, I bet you had a lot of fun in that car. That car was your ticket to freedom.

I'm sure you went on all sorts of adventures with your friends in that car.

This is the type of massive gratitude that will give you more gifts from the Universe. Some may say, "If I appreciated my old clunker, the Universe would just give me more old clunkers!" Sorry, but the Universe isn't a spiteful bitch. The Universe loves you and wants what's best for you. The Universe knows perfectly well you don't want an old clunker of a car. It already knows what you want. It just wants to be sure you can appreciate all the things you do have and all the things you've had in the past.

Just put yourself in the Universe's shoes. I will ask this question again. Would you instead give gifts to someone who keeps asking for new gifts—thereby not appreciating the current and past gifts…or would you rather give gifts to someone who has enjoyed all the gifts that you gave in the past?

The answer is obvious.

So, what I do—and what I recommend to everyone—is to take those seven minutes that it takes to fall asleep and appreciate all that you have now. Appreciate all that you have had in the past without going down some sad memory lane. You must have an upbeat, positive appreciation.

Having an upbeat, positive appreciation means that you are happy with your current life. Don't worry; the Universe is not going to deny you stuff because you are entirely satisfied with your life now. The Universe knows you want more stuff. You just must show a massive appreciation for what you already have.

Sadly, too many people get hung up on this. They think if they give up asking for stuff that the Universe will cancel their order. It's not true. I gave up asking to find someone that would be marriage material. The Universe didn't cancel my order because I stopped asking. It knew what I really wanted—and always wanted. I just wanted to see if I was really appreciating and enjoying my life as it was. And I was. When I let go and stopped asking, it was probably one of the happiest days of my life.

It's important to appreciate your past events and be okay that they are in the past. I would often miss my college days and lament that I was now living in the real world. It took me a long time to adopt a new attitude. Now, I think about my college days with joy, but I also recognize those were great days in the past, and my life is good now. I don't have nostalgic feelings about it. I have feelings of joy. I understand time marches on, and things change.

I also understand that the more I am enjoying my life, the more I will get to enjoy my life.

This works for everything. Let's take a look:

Weight loss

Instead of being disappointed about your weight. Appreciate a time when you were happy with your weight. If that time never existed, appreciate the efforts you (or your parents) put in to help you lose weight. Find something to enjoy.

If you had a good body in the past, instead of lamenting about how it is now, appreciate that you had it while you did. And understand that aging is a natural process. You will find this will lift a lot of blocks for you.

Money

Appreciate a time when you had money. You may have only found a few quarters in the sofa cushions. Appreciate that and recall the joy you had when you found those quarters so you could buy a burger at the local burger joint with your friends.

As mentioned earlier in this book, Andrew Carnegie, the multimillionaire steel magnate, relished the very first raise he ever got. Even though it was only for a few dollars a month. In his autobiography that he had written a few years before his death at 83, Carnegie said that the meager raise at his young age meant more to him than all the millions he had acquired over his lifetime. I'm sure his appreciation of that meager wage when he was young contributed to his abundant life.

Love

Appreciate past relationships. Obviously, if it was a previous relationship, it was one that didn't work out. However, appreciate the things about the relationship that you did enjoy. Every relationship has had its bright spots; otherwise, the relationship would have only lasted a few seconds. Not much of a relationship there. It's important to remember every one of those relationships and recall the good times you had.

I believe this is what helped me to manifest my wife. Not only had I stopped asking (by setting a new course for myself), but I unconsciously appreciated my past relationships. In other words, subconsciously, I was saying, "I've had my fill with all my past relationships. I don't need any more now."

Career

Look at every career move as a steppingstone of where you are now. Many of us have had many lousy jobs. And many of us have had that dream job that fizzled away through no fault of our own. The point here is not to lament a past job that we had found so enjoyable.

You want to appreciate the opportunity that you did have that job. And maybe the reason you no longer have that job is that you didn't appreciate that job. I know this has happened to me more times than I care to think. Take time now to really appreciate that job. Now is the time to communicate to the Universe that you really did appreciate that job.

You don't need to do anymore asking. You just need to do more appreciating and having gratitude for what you have now and what you have had in the past.

What I said about appreciating good jobs and bad jobs can also be applied to relationships. You've had good ones and bad ones. And some have fizzled through no fault of your own. You can still appreciate them with a high level of emotion—hopefully, love and joy, and not anger or revenge.

House gratitude inventory

Walk around your house and appreciate everything you have. If you don't enjoy something, then it might be time to get rid of it.

I love walking around my home and appreciating everything I have. If I ever get to the point where I don't really appreciate something, I find a way to discard it. I will usually give it to charity or take it to the dump.

9. Stop checking in

This one was a biggie for me. When you are manifesting something into your life, there is a tendency to keep checking in to see if it arrived.

I recognized this bad habit when I was looking for a new job. I would check my email or Linked In to see if "anything happened." The only time I got offers for interviews was when I stopped checking in and was completely doing something else.

If I were checking my email for correspondence from a friend, that was when I would get an email about a job offer. When I constantly checked my email for job offers, nothing came.

So, I learned to stop checking in. However, it's not as easy as it seems. Not checking in doesn't just mean not checking email or social media. It also means stop checking in in your mind.

You can't fake not checking in. You may resist checking your email or your email because you know you shouldn't be "checking in." However, that is not enough. You must completely check out. Your mind must be completely checked out. You must busy yourself with some other task, so your mind isn't checking in.

The most successful people who make lots of money only check their emails and voicemails twice a day. They know that checking in all time is a big distraction and is a form of asking. They keep their minds off it by staying busy doing other things.

You don't want to be constantly asking. Your checking into social media and email is asking the Universe for things to be different. You are saying that you are not satisfied with how things are now.

This doesn't mean you can never check email or social media. What I mean is checking those for the sake of passing the time or trying to make yourself feel better will keep your manifestations away from you.

Conclusion

All these exercises are designed to raise your vibration with the Universe. They are designed to instill in your unconscious mind that everything is good with you now and that you are open to receive more goodness.

These exercises are not meant to be taken as a step-by-step guide. There is no right or wrong way to do these. It all comes down to your belief system.

I find doing these exercises allows me to have a stronger belief in what I am doing and have a greater appreciation for the life I have.

Key Takeaways:

- Keep a journal of wins to increase your confidence
- Keep a journal of magic to heighten your belief
- Appreciate all things you've had in the past and in the present
- Enjoy life now and believe that everything is going your way

- Stop checking in (to see if what you want is coming to you).

Conclusion

I've written a lot about affirmations and visualizations. My personal feeling on those is that they work as long as you know and believe these tools are designed to change how you feel. They are not there to tap into the Universe. You are the Universe.

The way the Universe works is that you cannot be attached to the outcome. You must be okay with whatever happens. It's okay to want something and try to manifest it into your life. However, you must be okay with the outcome, whether it's good or bad.

This is why I advocate coming up with a worst-case scenario when trying to manifest something extraordinary in your life. You are telling the Universe that you do not lack anything, and everything is okay with you. You take the desperation out of the equation.

You must have a firm belief in yourself more than the tools that you use. The tools are there to get you to believe in yourself. Don't get caught up in whether you are using the tools correctly. There is no wrong or correct way to use any kind of manifestation tool. It's all about you being in alignment with the Universe—which is you!

You were meant for something huge

Think about all the successful people in the world. Are they any more special than you? They may seem unusual because they have more money and fame. But they are just ordinary people who breathe the same oxygen that you do. You must believe that you are meant for something extraordinary.

Once you start to believe that you are destined for something extraordinary, you can do anything. I know it sounds like a lot of feel-good mumbo jumbo. But it's true. You don't need any ideas right now, and you don't need any opportunities right now. You don't need any money right now, either. You just need to believe that you are destined for greatness and that you are ready to take action.

And that greatness can be anything. You can decide you want to be the greatest wife in the world. You can choose to be the best grass cutter in the world. You can choose to be the best customer service person in the world. You can decide to be the best barber in the world. You can choose to be the best bartender in the world. Whatever you choose, you will see great things come to you if you decide that you are destined for greatness and act toward that goal.

But don't worry; you won't have to take massive action. You just need to decide that you will take action. That is all that is required for great things to come to you.

One final thought

Don't mess with the Universe. Don't "experiment" with this manifestation stuff. It could come back to haunt you. In previous chapters, I had mentioned that I had—on a whim—asked for some money. I didn't need the money, but I asked for it anyway.

I ended up getting it. However, there was a time when I asked for money on a whim that completely backfired on me. As an experiment, I asked the Universe for $7,800 to see if the Universe was listening to me.

It was. It made sure that my bank account was $7,800 lighter. My refrigerator had died the day after I had asked "on a whim" for $7,800. What was the total cost of a new refrigerator? You guessed it: $7,830, to be exact. The Universe was listening.

While I was pissed that my refrigerator broke and I had to shell out $7,830 for a new one, I was happy that the Universe was listening to me. I learned my lesson. Don't mess with the Universe.

I hope you enjoy the journey as much as I have. Good luck to you!

Thank you for reading this book! If you want to reach out to me with any questions and concerns, please email me at
AustinWintergreen@gmail.com

May I ask you a small favor?

If you enjoyed reading this book and would like other people to benefit from the information in this book, could you please review my book on Amazon and Goodreads?

Thank you!

Printed in Great Britain
by Amazon